If you're a believer, it's hard not to be ~~arrogant. I have a t-shirt that~~ reads on the front, 'Jesus likes me mo *Bless-ed – 52 Weekly Blessings You Ha Your Lost Friends Find Theirs*, Larry wonderful way, reminds us about how are. Then you have to deal with the a as Dr. Dixon says, it's all God and Hi give you joy in your faith and, at the see others get the t-shirt and to join you in the dance.

STEVE BROWN
Founder and Bible Teacher, Key Life Network,
Author, *Laughter and Lament: The Radical Freedom of Joy and Sorrow*

Larry Dixon presents us with a book that is easy and entertaining to read. It has a theological depth that belies its folksy feel. Each chapter is liberally graced with Scripture references that provide a sound basis for the many blessings presented. Filled with many little anecdotes, Larry's writing constantly refers to the text of Scripture as a basis for its content. *Bless-ed* is based on sound biblical principles and careful use of the text of Scripture.

PHILIP BOOM
President of Emmaus Bible College, Dubuque, Iowa

Larry Dixon has done it again! As a well-trained and experienced theologian, he has taken truth and presented it in such a clear and winsome way that the 'man on the street' can easily understand. Theologically, he 'puts the cookies on the lower shelf' within reach of all of us. Larry's amazing sense of humor puts us readers at ease, but he never shrinks back from talking about things that may be difficult and hard for some of us to hear. In a very real sense, this book is a buy-one-get-one: not only does it artfully articulate many of the blessings that we believers have in Christ, but it also helps us know how to 'translate' those blessings into meaningful witnessing conversations with the non-Christian 'Mikes' in our lives. And yes, I have some 'Mikes' in my life for whom I am burdened, and this book is definitely helping me reach out to them more effectively. Larry's writing is both doctrinal and practical; it's convicting and encouraging. If you're like me, you won't be able to wait and read only one chapter per week; you'll want to read the whole book much more quickly than that because of its edifying and equipping contents.

GEORGE W. MURRAY
Former President and Chancellor of Columbia International
University, Columbia, South Carolina

How we need to share Christ with our friends – naturally and effectively! I never read a book like this without being motivated and helped. In this personal account, Larry Dixon describes his earnest attempts to share the Gospel with a friend and how we can be encouraged to do the same. His short, practical lessons will provide you with next steps and ongoing zeal. Thank you, Larry Dixon!

ROBERT J. MORGAN
Author, *The Red Sea Rules* and *Then Sings My Soul*;
Teaching Pastor, The Donelson Fellowship, Nashville, Tennessee

Retired theology professor Larry Dixon has written a helpful book that is sure to encourage believers in Christ. He includes fifty-two short 'Blessings' that Christians may have forgotten. He follows them up with 'Action Steps' that help us put the truth to work in our lives. Noteworthy is the author's heart for the lost which comes through on every page. Here is good book to use for devotions that will stimulate the head, heart, and hands and feet!

ROBERT A. PETERSON
Theologian, editor, and co-author, *Jesus In Prophecy: How Christ's Life Fulfills Biblical Predictions*

Dr. Larry Dixon is the most actively evangelistic theologian that I know. He is relentless in seeking non-Christian friends through tennis, chess, correspondence, and whoever he bumps into in order to share the good news of the Gospel. Larry has written this book to encourage Christians to truly know what they have in Christ, as a way of life, and as discussion starters with their non-Christian friends. Using profound quotes, gentle humor, extensive biblical passages, along with recommended readings and suggestions for prayer, these blessings will not only be a strong reminder of what we have, but, if lived out, will make your Christianity contagious to those without Christ. The 52 chapters cover such topics as Joy, Forgiveness, Heaven, Sexuality, and even How to Grow Old. They will not only make for inspiring reading and studying but good sermon material as well.

ALLAN MCKECHNIE
Professor Emeritus
Columbia International University,
Columbia, South Carolina

One of the things I love most about Larry Dixon's books is they are supremely practical. He takes Scripture and theological concepts and presents them in ways that anyone can understand. His most recent work is yet another example. I am a pastor and am often asked about resources for small groups – this book now makes my list of recommendations. Every chapter includes action steps which are great exercises for spiritual growth. Those who read this book will enjoy it and be challenged by the faith lessons Dr. Dixon shares. The readings are short, which is great for people like me with a short attention span, however the content is theologically rich. Prepare to be Bless-ed.

JEFF PHILPOTT
Sandhills Community Church

This book is very helpful for Christians who like to please God in their daily activities – especially for those who have the burden to reach their lost friends. We have studied the book *Bless-ed* with our Monday Bible school students and it was very sharpening for their understanding. I will recommend this book to Christians who love to serve Christ, especially to my Ethiopian Christian believers, to read it and benefit from it.

MULUGETA ASHAGRE ENDESHAW
East African Director of T-NET International,
Former General Secretary, Ethiopian Christian Brethren Church

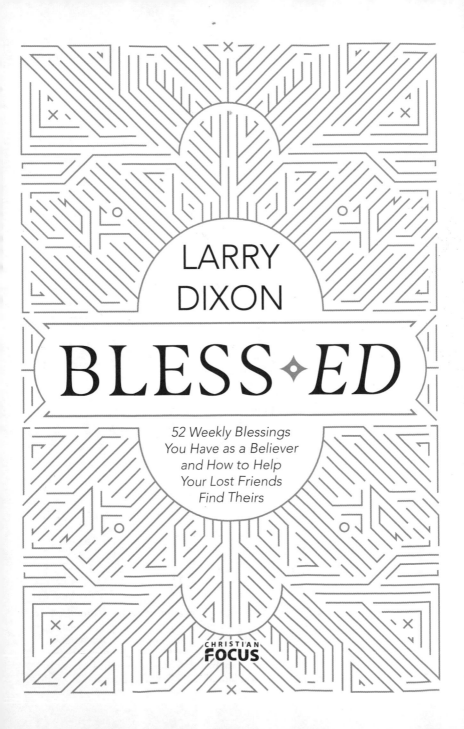

LARRY
DIXON

BLESS·ED

*52 Weekly Blessings
You Have as a Believer
and How to Help
Your Lost Friends
Find Theirs*

CHRISTIAN
FOCUS

Copyright © Larry Dixon 2023

paperback ISBN 978-1-5271-0977-3
ebook ISBN 978-1-5271-1032-8

10 9 8 7 6 5 4 3 2 1

Published in 2023
by
Christian Focus Publications Ltd,
Geanies House, Fearn, Ross-shire,
IV20 1TW, Great Britain.

www.christianfocus.com

Cover design by
Rubner Durais

Printed by Bell & Bain, Glasgow

like 'it just *went North*' or 'it *went West*'? Is it just because we lost the Civil War?

I occasionally see someone wearing a T-shirt that says 'Too Blessed to Be Stressed!' I'm glad they're coping with life, and that their clothing helps them do so, but I wonder what they mean exactly. What does it mean to be 'blessed'?

A Word about the Title: And while I think about it, I need to explain how I've written this book's title. You see, there are two ways to pronounce this word 'blessed.' There's the one syllable way ('blessed'). For example, someone might respond to the question 'How you doin'?' with 'I'm blessed.' There's also the two syllable way ('bless-ed'). For example, my Roman Catholic friends speak of the 'Bless-ed Mary.' It's this two syllable way of using the term 'blessed' that I would like to emphasize in this book: 'Bless-ed.' Two syllables. It just sounds more spiritual, more holy, and more, well, desirable.

So, I would ask that the title be read in the two-syllable way 'Bless-ed ...' Some might think we are trying to bless someone named 'Ed,' but that's certainly not the case. One can easily see that the '-ed' isn't capitalized, right? And we're really not talking about Ed, but about my friend Mike.

My Motivation: You need to know a bit of why I've written this book. The central character in this book *is* my friend 'Mike' (not his real name. You can tell that by the quote marks which I'll use just this once).

I came to know Mike as a result of one of my trips from South Carolina to New Jersey to speak in a church. This church invited me to come for ten days to speak on

INTRODUCTION

I'm from 'down South.' I was taught to be nice to people, to ask them how they are, to address them with 'yes, sir' and 'no, sir' and 'yes, ma'm' and 'no, ma'm.' I'm slowly realizing that most men don't care about the yes-sir's and the no-sir's and most ladies get mad because they think those expressions imply that they look as old as their gray-haired mothers.

We have a number of Southern sayings which I sometimes use, such as, 'Bless your heart!' and 'He's so precious!' and 'Ya'll come by and see us sometime.' To be quite honest, those expressions are sometimes insincere. We once in a while use the words 'Bless your heart' more like a curse than a blessing. 'He's so precious' can mean he's a few fries short of a Happy Meal, and, if they show up uninvited to our home, we wonder why they are there (even though we gave them a clear invitation with the expression 'Ya'll come by and see us sometime.').

By the way, I get a little upset when I hear someone say about a situation, 'It just *went South* really quickly!' They're using my geographical location (my home) as a term of disaster and catastrophe. Why not say something

Contents

two successive Sundays and to meet with their leadership team to work together.

I am an avid tennis player. Notice – I did not say a good one. But I went to a local tennis club in NJ and met a really good player in his eighties (I turned seventy-two in February). Mike has played in national tournaments and he and I got together to play tennis each time I made the trek to NJ.

Mike was kind enough to take the short survey I used in my *Unlike Jesus* book[1] about people who are 'still on their way' to faith. With his permission, I included his response to my questions in my book – and my response to his response. I have prayed for my friend Mike's salvation almost every day without fail. You need to know that I try to be very careful in witnessing to those I know will be long-term or even lifelong friends.

On a recent visit to NJ, Mike arranged for me to play tennis with a few of his friends and I began praying for an opportunity to share the gospel with him afterwards. I felt that he was a bit offended by my referring to him (without using his name, of course) in my book as 'lost' and 'unsaved.'

We chatted briefly on the last day I could get together with him. I apologized to him for offending him with my language of 'lost' and 'unsaved' (without denying the truth of his condition before God) and he said, 'Well, you're certainly entitled to your opinion, Larry! Don't worry about me. I'm fine!' But if the Bible is true, he could not be more wrong.

---

1. Larry Dixon, *Unlike Jesus: Let's Stop Unfriending the World* (Gonzalez, Florida: Energion Publications, 2019).

I was also able to say to him that the Lord is the answer to his loneliness (his wife passed away two years ago). And that was it. I'll keep in touch with him and pray for him each day.

But this friendship got me thinking about what I have as a believer and what my unsaved friends *don't* have. I am certainly not gloating in what I enjoy as a follower of Jesus. But Mike has me pondering the blessings I have as a Christian.

So this book has two purposes: (1) I want to become more aware of some of the blessings I have as a believer and (2) I want to become more intentional in helping Mike find those same blessings for himself.

The Structure of This Book: This book has fifty-two short chapters. The reader may read one chapter each Monday or read the whole book at once. Each chapter will discuss a blessing that the believer in Jesus enjoys – or *should* enjoy. Relevant biblical passages will be recommended for study during the particular week. We will also suggest some solid Christian books that will be helpful as well as some activities for the week.

But we will also talk about how someone like the Mike in your life doesn't enjoy that blessing – *and what you can do about it.* We will offer specific action steps you can take to help your Mike, especially emphasizing how you can pray for God the Holy Spirit to speak to his or her heart.

But let me ask an incredibly important question: *Got a Mike in your life?* Are you aware of the many blessings, starting with salvation, that your Mike doesn't enjoy? But, before we begin our look at that list, let's think about the blessings that Mike *does* have!

PREFACE:
Already Bless-ed

We'll begin looking at the fifty-two blessings you have as a believer (and your lost friend needs) in a moment, but we first need to remind ourselves of the blessings your lost friend already enjoys.

The Bible is quite clear that *life itself* is the blessing of God. He is the Creator of life; Scripture says that He 'gives life to everything' (1 Tim. 6:13). And even the most belligerent of unbelievers has life from God. They may not acknowledge it or may try to explain it away evolutionarily, but there it is. Life. From the Creator. Revelation 4:11 says, 'for you created all things, and by your will they were created and have their being.'

In Acts 17, the Apostle Paul engages with five very different groups of unbelievers. Paul is greatly disturbed, as he waits for his friends in Athens, to see the city overrun by idols. And so he preaches the gospel. But first, he engages intellectually with the five groups: the Jews, the God-fearing Greeks, some Epicurean and Stoic philosophers, and a group I call the intellectual loiterers who just happened to be there (Acts 17:16-18).

Paul's approach is amazing for he shockingly *compliments* these groups for their religiosity and then uses their altar to an unknown god as a touchpoint for talking about the real God. There is so much in this chapter worth investigating, but one point stands out: in his presentation of the gospel, Paul emphasizes the uniqueness of the one true God and says that 'he himself gives everyone life and breath and everything else' (v. 25). We read of the Lord in Psalm 145:16, 'You open your hand and satisfy the desires of every living thing.' That's the providential care of the Creator for every human being on the planet!

Your unsaved friend may not admit it, but his or her very next breath is a gift of the Creator. He is the One who 'causes his sun to rise on the evil and the good, and sends rain on the righteous and the unrighteous' (Matt. 5:45). Both the sunrise and rainfall indiscriminately bless the unbeliever – whether he or she recognizes these gifts or not.

So, when we think of our Mikes and their lost condition before God, we need to remind ourselves of the numerous blessings they already enjoy even outside the family of God! When your lost friend welcomes a new baby into his family, when they watch a multi-colored sunrise over the ocean, when they feel the pelting raindrops after a drought, they ought to thank their Creator for His mercies. They are not bereft of blessings. Those blessings are bestowed on them without their permission, but, sadly, also often without their acknowledgement. And that's where we believers come in.

I have a good friend who is a master scuba diver. He has traveled the world and plumbed the depths of far-flung oceans in his life. His pictures of exotic sea creatures are quite impressive. He's invited me to take up scuba diving, but I've no intention of becoming some shark's lunch!

However, my friend is far from God. He enjoys the beauties of God's oceans but, as far as I know, gives God no credit for His breathtaking creativity. He does not worship the One who made these amazing water-dwellers. He enjoys the benefits of the Creator's work without acknowledging the Creator. And that grieves me. We can specify these blessings as finding their source in a providentially kind Creator who loves His creation and sustains it by His mercy.

Sometimes, we Jesus followers speak when we shouldn't and are mute when we ought to express our gratitude to the Lord for His providential blessings. I learned long ago that my job is not to rebuke my lost friends who use God's name in vain, but *I* need to be rebuked for not praising His name (publicly!) for His goodness to His creation. In a culture that seems to say whatever it wants whenever it wishes, we believers need to vocalize the truth of God's blessings on 'the righteous' and 'the wicked.'

Life, and breath, and everything else. Those blessings are indeed enjoyed by my friend Mike – but without a saving relationship to Jesus Christ.

Let's begin our thinking about the blessings you and I should enjoy and how we can help those outside Christ find them.

The Blessing of a Final Authority for One's Beliefs

I have made a covenant with God that he sends me neither visions, dreams, nor even angels. I am well satisfied with the gift of the Holy Scriptures which give me abundant instruction and all that I need to know both for this life and for that which is to come (Martin Luther).[1]

Why do you believe what you believe? What is your authority for what you choose to incorporate into your view of the world? Some people trust their reason; some their emotions. Others rely on some religious authority to tell them what to believe. I heard about a man who was asked, 'What do you believe?' 'I believe what my church believes,' he replied. 'Well,' asked the friend, 'what does your church believe?' 'The church believes what I believe!' 'That's interesting,' said the

---

1. James Swan, 'Luther: Denying Sola Scriptura With An Unbiblical Understanding of the Word "Prophet"?' Beggars All: Reformation and Apologetics. July 20, 2007. https://beggarsallreformation.blogspot.com/2007/07/luther-denying-sola-scriptura-with.html.

friend. 'What do you and your church believe?' The man thought for a moment, then replied, '*We believe the same thing, dummy!*'

For the believer in Jesus, there's a better authority for what we are to believe – and it's the Word of God.

WE HAVE A FINAL AUTHORITY FOR WHAT WE BELIEVE!

The Blessing

My friend Mike doesn't 'feel' like he's lost or unsaved. For many people, their feelings are their final authority for what they believe. As a follower of Jesus, my authority is God's Word, the Bible. And the Bible is quite clear in declaring the human person's lostness before a holy, Triune God.

The Bible

The Bible (composed of sixty-six books) claims to be the Word of God. This isn't a unique claim to Christianity, but there are good reasons to trust the Bible rather than other pretend authorities (such as the *Book of Mormon*, or the *Koran*, or *Science and Health with Key to the Scriptures*). God's Word promises to be a light to our path (Ps. 119:105), a treasure of truth to one's mind (Ps. 19:7-11), nourishing food for one's life (Job 23:12), and even a double-edged sword piercing one's soul for good (Heb. 4:12). Martin Luther confessed: 'The Bible is alive, it speaks to me; it has feet, it runs after me; it has hands, it lays hold on me.'

For many people their final authority for what they believe is their heart. When we lived in Canada, my good friend John (who professed to be a believer) asked if I would talk to his brother Nick who believed everything, it seemed, except Christianity. I asked Nick what his authority was for what he believed and he said, 'My heart. If I read something that resonates with me, I add it to my belief system.' He then said to me, 'Larry, what do you think about my practice?' I said with a smile, 'Nick, I'm not sure you want to hear what I really think. And I want to stay friends with you.' He said, 'No, really. I want to know what you think.' I then said, 'Nick, Jeremiah 17:9 says that our hearts are deceitful and desperately wicked and that we should not trust our hearts as our final authority for what we believe.' I don't believe Nick and I talked about spiritual things much after that, but I told him the truth.

This issue of the Bible's final authority for one's life cannot be overstated. If the Bible is the very Word of God – and there are abundant evidences to affirm that conviction wholeheartedly – then it must have daily power over my decisions, actions, motivations, feelings, priorities, etc.

ACTION STEPS

1. For you as a believer, thank the Lord for God's Word, your final authority for what you are to believe. Write out a new prayer every day this week expressing your gratitude for the Scriptures.

2. A bit of homework: Read through Psalm 119 over this week and list at least fifty benefits of the Word of God in your life.

3. For extra reading, I recommend buying either a *One Year Bible* or a *Two Year Bible* and committing yourself to reading through all of God's Word in either one or two years.

4. Pray today for your lost friend, that he or she might become interested in what the Bible says about life and salvation and the world. Ask God the Holy Spirit to bring a godly conviction to their soul. Consider praying about offering a one-on-one Bible study to your friend.

The Blessing of the Assurance of Forgiveness

In the shadow of my hurt, forgiveness feels like a decision to reward my enemy. But in the shadow of the cross, forgiveness is merely a gift from one undeserving soul to another. Forgiveness is the gift that insures my freedom from a prison of bitterness and resentment. When I accept forgiveness from God, I'm free from the penalty of my sin. When I extend forgiveness to my adversary, there's a sense in which I am set free from his sin as well (Andy Stanley).[1]

I've been thinking recently about what believers in Jesus have and what my unsaved friends *don't* have in not knowing the Lord Jesus as their Savior. My friend Mike chooses to think of himself as not lost, as not being outside the family of God.

Please don't misunderstand me. Mike is a great guy. He is giving, kind, compassionate, but utterly deceived

---

1. Andy Stanley, *Enemies of the Heart: Breaking Free from the Four Emotions That Control You* (Colorado Springs: Multnomah Books, 2006), p. 129.

about his status before a holy God. And therefore, I'm so thankful for God's Word telling me the truth about my need of a Savior. A Savior who can forgive me.

I heard one man say, 'I don't mind forgiving and forgetting. I just don't want the one I'm forgiving to forget that he has been forgiven.' The blessing we want to focus on today is that of having our sins taken care of by Jesus on the cross. For, when I think of what we have in Christ ...

WE HAVE THE ASSURANCE OF FORGIVENESS!

The Blessing

How audacious of Christians to claim their sins have been eternally forgiven by God, that they are now in His family, and that He will never turn away from them! But that's what the Bible, God's Word, promises to all who turn to Him in faith.

Unfortunately, few in our world seem concerned about their sin and God's holiness. Someone has said that Jonathan Edwards' sermon, 'Sinners in the Hands of an Angry God' has been twisted today into 'God in the Hands of Angry Sinners'! God's Spirit brings conviction of sin which, upon belief in the gospel, leads to complete and righteous forgiveness from a holy God.

The Bible

Because the Bible is our final authority for what we believe, we can be assured of our permanent forgiveness by God. We read that it is in Christ ,in whom we have redemption, the *forgiveness* of sins' (Col. 1:14, emphasis added). We can be thankful with the psalmist who declares, 'But with you there is *forgiveness*, so that we can, with reverence, serve you' (Ps. 130:4, emphasis added). We learn that the Lord Jesus came for sinners 'to open their eyes and turn them from darkness to light, and from the power of Satan to God, so that they may receive *forgiveness* of sins and a place among those who are sanctified by faith in [Christ]' (Acts 26:18, emphasis added). Even the prophets spoke about the coming Savior 'that everyone who believes in him receives *forgiveness* of sins through his name' (Acts 10:43, emphasis added). But the hard fact is that forgiveness is found only in Christ. And if one doesn't have *Him*, one doesn't have *it*.

ACTION STEPS

1. A bit of homework: Interview five Christian friends this week on what it means to be forgiven by God. Take a few notes on your conversations. Discuss what you've learned with your spouse or a good friend.

2. Sometimes we need to use new words because we've become accustomed to the old words. Write out a paragraph of praise to the Lord for your forgiveness in Christ without using words like 'forgiveness' or 'saved' or 'redeemed.' You might consider sharing that paragraph with an unsaved friend. Blame me for the assignment! But ask them if your paragraph makes sense to them.

3. Consider ordering and reading my short booklet on salvation entitled *Saved: Rescued from God, by God, and for God* found on amazon.com at: shorturl.at/bqN18.

Just type in that url (shorturl.at/bqN18) into your search engine.

4. PRAYER: Pray specifically for your unsaved friend this week that he would be open to the Spirit's work of convicting him of his need of Christ. Pray about the possibility of sharing your paragraph (of Action Step #2) with him.

⇀ BLESSING 3 ↼

The Blessing of a Burdened Heart

If you really want to receive joy and happiness, then serve
others with all your heart. Lift their burden, and your own
burden will be lighter (Ezra Taft Benson).[1]

The believer in Christ has so many blessings. And
my unsaved friend Mike is helping me to 'count
my blessings.' I've been thinking about what I enjoy as
a follower of Jesus. Sadly, my lost friends, although they
enjoy much by way of God's providential care (common
grace), there are some blessings they don't yet have.

There's a rather strange one that believers have and it is –

WE HAVE THE BLESSING OF
A BURDENED HEART!

The Blessing

I am not suggesting that my unsaved friends don't weep
at the death of a loved one, or agonize over poor life-
choices that their children make, or that they aren't

---

1. Quoted in Addittya Tamhankar, Beauty of Acceptance (Chandigarh,
India: White Falcon Publishing, 2020), p. 25.

concerned with the many faces of evil in our world. But I think those 'burdens' are the result of being made in the image of God, not necessarily of being a new creation in Christ. For someone considering Christianity, I am tempted to say to them, 'Buckle up! Get ready to get your heart burdened!'

The Bible

The classic passage on becoming a burden-bearer, I think, is Matthew 11:28-30 where the Lord Jesus says,

> Come to me, all you who are weary and burdened, and I will give you rest. Take my yoke upon you and learn from me, for I am gentle and humble in heart, and you will find rest for your souls. For my yoke is easy and my burden is light.

A burdened heart is actually a healthy heart, *if* the burden is of Christ. Prior to receiving Christ as our Savior, there is a weariness and a burdenness (new word!) that can only be remedied by the rest that He gives. If 'I will give you rest' refers to salvation, then it is critical to see that the believer after conversion has work to do (a yoke to wear) and learning to pursue.

A burdened heart looks out at the world and weeps. G. K. Chesterton put it this way: 'Do not free a camel of the burden of his hump; you may be freeing him from being a camel.'[2] We were created to be burdened.

A burdened heart looks at friends and family without Christ ... and prays! It looks at itself and asks not that the burden be taken away but that it be increased, trusting

---

2. G. K. Chesterton, *Orthodoxy: The Fundamentalist Argument* (MSAC Philosophy Group; First Neural Library Edition, January 26, 2008), p. 30.

God to work in His way. We read in Galatians 6:1-5 the following:

> Brothers and sisters, if someone is caught in a sin, you who live by the Spirit should restore that person gently. But watch yourselves, or you also may be tempted. Carry each other's burdens, and in this way you will fulfill the law of Christ. If anyone thinks they are something when they are not, they deceive themselves. Each one should test their own actions. Then they can take pride in themselves alone, without comparing themselves to someone else, for each one should carry their own load.

Please notice that this section is directed at 'you who live by the Spirit.' It would be easy for someone to say, 'I'm not really living by the Spirit, so I don't have to seek to restore a brother or sister who is caught in sin!' No! We are supposed to be living by the Spirit so that we *can* help a fallen comrade!

Notice we are to 'carry each other's burdens' and by so doing we will 'fulfill the law of Christ' (v. 2). But there is individual responsibility as well: 'each one should carry their own load' (v. 5).

ACTION STEPS

1. Would you say your heart is *burdened* for someone else? How would you fill in the following blank? 'I believe Jesus has given me a burden to carry and it is _____.'

2. Let one or two fellow believers know this week that you want to pray for their burdens. Share with them a burden you are carrying for yourself.

3. If you are a parent or a grandparent, you will find great profit in reading Stormie Omartian's book *Praying for Your Adult Children*.

4. Pray for your lost friend that he or she will become burdened for their salvation. And pray for yourself to become more burdened for his or her coming to Christ.

⤜ BLESSING 4 ⤛

The Blessing of a Proper View of Suffering

The believer in God must explain one thing, the existence of suffering; the nonbeliever, however, must explain the existence of everything else (*The Nine Questions People Ask About Judaism*).[1]

Ithank the Lord for my friend Mike. He does not know the Lord – yet – as his Savior, but God is using him to remind me of the many blessings which I have 'in Christ.' This study is multi-faceted and is helping me enormously in taking stock of what I have as a follower of Jesus. And I purpose not simply to coast through my Christian life, oblivious to the many gifts which being in God's family has given me.

The next 'blessing' we want to consider might seem odd, but it is a really critical one. This is a broken world. We are broken as people: terrible tragedies and catastrophes happen on this planet (and to us) under the watchful eye

---

1. Dennis Prager and Joseph Telushkin, *The Nine Questions People Ask About Judaism* (New York: Touchstone; Reprint edition, April 21, 1986), p. 27.

of a sovereign God. How are we to understand pain and tragedy? Thankfully, as believers in Christ –

WE POSSESS A PROPER VIEW OF SUFFERING!

The Blessing

The Bible does not sugar-coat this world's fallenness with all its effects of 'natural disasters' (earthquakes, tsunamis, hurricanes, etc.) and man-made evil (crime, betrayal, anger, revenge, injustice, prejudice, greed, etc.). But how are we to understand this world's suffering in light of the Bible's picture of a God of love?

Scholars refer to this effort at understanding evil as a *theodicy* (a defense of God's justice in the face of evil's reality). Some religious systems deny the reality of evil (the cult Christian Science is an example), compromise God's omnipotence or omniscience (Rabbi Harold Kushner's *When Bad Things Happen to Good People* is an example of the former; Greg Boyd's open theism an example of the latter), or resign themselves to a kind of deterministic fatalism about evil (Islam is an example of this approach).

The Bible

The Bible provides the very best theodicy, for it affirms the real existence of evil and suffering while setting forth the goodness and justice of the biblical God. And God's Word does not hesitate to show us godly people who had wrong views about suffering. One thinks of Job and his friends who were sure either Job had sinned greatly (and deserved what he was getting) or God was unfairly making Job His target (and needed to be sued in court for His [God's] mistake). Even Jesus' disciples cut to the chase theologically and thought the man-born-blind's condition was because of sin (either his or his parents). Jesus corrects them by saying that 'this happened so that the works of God would be displayed in his life' (John 9:3).

As God-manifest-in-the-flesh, Jesus allows death to take his friend Lazarus, even though He had the power to keep him from dying (John 11). I've worked on this passage and entitled it 'Friends Don't Let Friends ... Die!' But Jesus did.

One classic text on the issue of evil and suffering is Luke 13:1-5 where we read:

> Now there were some present at that time who told Jesus about the Galileans whose blood Pilate had mixed with their sacrifices. Jesus answered, 'Do you think that these Galileans were worse sinners than all the other Galileans because they suffered this way? I tell you, no! But unless you repent, you too will all perish. Or those eighteen who died when the tower in Siloam fell on them – do you think they were more guilty than all the others living in Jerusalem? I tell you, no! But unless you repent, you too will all perish.'

This brief theodicy by the Lord Jesus covers two areas of suffering and evil in our world. Notice *the victims of a vicious crime* in verses 1-3. Notice also *the victims of a violent accident* in verses 4-5. Neither the sin of the Galileans nor the guilt of those killed by the falling tower was the cause of their catastrophe. One man's depravity (Pilate's) and one tower's gravity illustrate a basic fact: *life is dangerous! Make sure you are right with God!*

ACTION STEPS

1. A bit of homework: There is much more in God's Word that prepares us for suffering. See such texts as: 2 Corinthians 1:5-7; Philippians 1:29; 3:10; Colossians 1:24; I Thessalonians 1:6; 2 Thessalonians 1:5; 2 Timothy 1:8; 2:3; Hebrews 2:18; 10:34; James 5:10; all of 1 Peter; Revelation 1:9; 2:10. Take some notes on these passages this week.

2. Interview a believing friend this week who is going through severe suffering (cancer, the loss of a loved one, marital unfaithfulness). Ask them carefully what God is teaching them in their trial. Then offer to pray with them.

3. Read the excellent book by Chris Tiegreen entitled *Why a Suffering World Makes Sense*. Perhaps offer a small group study of the book in your church.

4. PRAYER: Pray for yourself to live a life of faith even in the midst of trials and pain. And ask the Holy Spirit to use whatever challenge comes in your friend's life that he might see his need of getting right with the Lord.

✣ BLESSING 5 ✦

The Blessing of a Lifelong Mission

> This is the true joy of life: the being used up for a purpose recognized by yourself to be a mighty one; being a force of nature instead of a feverish, selfish little clot of ailments and grievances, complaining that the world will not devote itself to making you happy (George Bernard Shaw).[1]

I've recently been challenged (by my time with my unsaved friend Mike) to think about what I have as a believer and what those who are lost *don't* have. This may seem like a strange exercise, but it has a way of focusing my prayers and my priorities to genuinely care about my lost friends.

In sharing the biblical truth with Mike that he is 'lost' and 'unsaved' without Jesus, he responded with his conviction that he was just fine with God. But that's not what God's Word says. Another blessing that we who know Christ have is this –

---

1. Christopher Wixson, *George Bernard Shaw: A Very Short Introduction* (Oxford, United Kingdom: Oxford University Press, 2020), p. 111.

WE HAVE A LIFELONG, SATISFYING MISSION IN LIFE!

What is my friend Mike's 'mission' in life? I suppose – if I were to ask him – he would probably say, 'I want to be a good person, help others, be kind and compassionate, and die with my family by my side.' Those are good values and ambitious goals – but is that what life is about?

The Blessing

What about knowing the living God? What about helping to rescue people from God's eternal wrath? What about sharing in any way possible the message of forgiveness and reconciliation that Jesus provides to those who believe? What about a life mission that will require all one's energy and resources and priorities and insight and purpose? That's what we believers have. And though at times it might seem like a burden, it is a blessing.

The Bible

Jesus prayed in John 17 for all who would follow Him. 'Now this is eternal life: that they know you, the only true God, and Jesus Christ, whom you have sent' (v. 3). He commissioned His disciples in Matthew 28:18-20 with the words:

> All authority in heaven and on earth has been given to me. Therefore go and make disciples of all nations, baptizing them in the name of the Father and of the Son and of the Holy Spirit, and teaching them to obey everything I have commanded you. And surely I am with you always, to the very end of the age.

Life's purpose is to know the Lord and life's mission (for those who believe) is to disciplize (my word) people everywhere to follow Jesus. This is the believer's lifelong, satisfying mission. There is none greater than this.

ACTION STEPS

Someone has said of the Christian, 'You are either a missionary or a mission field.' Believer, are you fully engaged in this Christ-given mission to reach the world? Some action steps you can take:

1. Read through the book of Acts this week taking special note of the passion and commitment of the early Christians to fulfill the Great Commission the Lord gave to them. Take a few notes and perhaps share what you've learned with a friend.

2. Interview a real-life missionary (either active or retired) some time this week. Ask them questions like, 'If you had to live your life over again, what would you do differently?' 'What lessons have you learned about your lifelong mission that can help other believers?'

3. Read John Piper's book *Don't Waste Your Life* and discuss it with a friend. Are there any points in that book with which you might disagree? Check out desiringgod.org for Piper's many resources.

4. PRAYER: To be quite honest and blunt, in the words of Pastor John Piper, my friend Mike has *wasted his life!* But it's not too late. And I pray he will come to Christ and use the remainder of his days to have a mission far greater than any he has ever dreamed of.

Are you concerned that your friend does not have God's eternal mission in life? Pray that the Holy Spirit will speak to his heart – and remind him that he only has *one* life. And it can count for God!

✢ BLESSING 6 ✦

The Blessing of Somewhere to Go with My Guilt

Guilt is regret for what we've done. Regret is guilt for what we didn't do (Mark Amend).[1]

My friend Mike has got me thinking about what I have as a believer and what those who are lost *don't* have. I can say without fear of contradiction – based on Mike's words – that he is indeed lost and won't (at this point) accept what God's Word says about him.

Let's consider another blessing that believers ought to appreciate and that is –

WE HAVE SOMEWHERE (BEYOND THIS WORLD) TO GO WITH OUR GUILT!

The Blessing

'Guilt is the thief of life', said the actor Anthony Hopkins. Of course, there's both legitimate and illegitimate guilt.

---

1. Quoted in Susan H. Lawrence, *Pure Emotion* (CreateSpace Independent Publishing Platform; 2nd edition, February 15, 2013), p. 169.

We often feel guilty about things that don't matter. And, more to the point, we seldom feel true guilt about the things that are of God and are of eternal significance. Someone has said, 'Never feel guilt while doing what's best for you.' The problem, of course, is that we often don't know what's best for us.

Biblical guilt is healthy and indicates that our conscience (molded by God's Word) is working! But we don't need to stay in our guilt. As one author says, 'We are not built for guilt, and it damages our souls and personalities – even our health.'

The Bible

God's Word has much to say about guilt. For example:

1. Some people are guilty of an eternal sin by blaspheming the Holy Spirit (Mark. 3:29). Is this sin possible today? Yes, in the sense that rejecting the Spirit's witness to the identity of Jesus excludes one from salvation.

2. Tragedies in life are not necessarily the result of personal sin or guilt (Luke 13:4). Violent accidents and vicious crimes are part of our broken world.

3. Guilt remains on those who claim they can see spiritually, but reject Christ (John 9:41). A lack of awareness of one's guilt doesn't eliminate one's responsibility.

4. Both Jesus' words and works condemn as guilty those who reject Him (John 15:22, 24). The evidence for the Person of Christ is irrefutable.

5. One who takes communion in an unworthy manner is guilty of sinning against the body and blood of the

Lord (1 Cor. 11:27). This is why many churches have a moment of reflection before they take the elements of the Lord's Supper.

6. The believer's heart of guilt can by cleansed by repentance and a faith in the Lord (Heb. 10:22). Psalm 32:5 says, 'And you forgave the guilt of my sin.'

7. Failing to keep one point of the law means one is guilty of breaking the whole law (James 2:10).

8. The Old Testament gives much material on what is called the guilt offering for sin (see Lev. 5).

I have a friend who recently completely rejected Christianity. He challenges the truthfulness of the Bible, the necessity of Christ's atoning work, the reality of the God of the Bible. I know of several quite serious sins that he has committed, hurting himself and others and grieving God in the process. At some point I want to ask him, 'What do you do with your guilt?'

The believer in the Lord Jesus has somewhere to go with his or her guilt. And that somewhere is a SOMEONE! Because our sins are forgiven by Christ, we can confess our shortcomings and ask for His restoration.

ACTION STEPS

1. Read over the verses mentioned above in the list this week. How would you define biblical guilt? How is biblical guilt a good thing?

2. Consider confessing to your unsaved friend something you have done or said for which you have found

forgiveness before the Lord. Explain why you are confident the Lord has forgiven you.

3. Read the following article 'What Does the Bible Say about Guilt?' found at Got Questions and email a friend some time this week about what you've learned.[2]

4. PRAYER: Pray for your friend to come under the conviction of the Holy Spirit. Pray that he would experience biblical guilt and ask your help in confessing his sin and trusting Christ.

---

2. https://www.gotquestions.org/Bible-guilt.html

⇢ BLESSING 7 ⇠

The Blessing of a Training Community

Seen on a church sign: 'This church is not full
of hypocrites. There's always room for more.'

I believe it is critical for the Christian to have unsaved friends. And one of the many benefits (other than being like Jesus, 'the friend of sinners') is that they remind us what *we* have in Christ that they don't yet have. My friend Mike got me thinking about what I have as a believer and what those who are lost *don't* have.

Asked about his status before God, Mike thinks he is just fine. But God's Word says we are lost and under God's judgment without Christ. However, after salvation, there is a world of learning to take place and a lot of training to undergo.

Let's think about a seventh benefit of the believer and it is that –

WE HAVE A COMMUNITY (BEING BUILT BY JESUS) WHERE WE CAN BE TRAINED TO DO GOD'S WORK!

The Blessing

Here, of course, we are talking about the local church. But it's important to remember that the believer in Jesus is part of the universal Body of Christ (another meaning of the term 'church'). And the local church is an expression of that universal Body.

The local church is not to be simply a gathering place of like-minded people. It is to be a training ground for serious disciples of the Savior.

Unfortunately, it seems that for many Jesus-followers today the local church has become optional. Some serve only when convenient, attend only when the weather is too bad to go to the lake, and contribute only when there's a bit of extra money or time. But that's not how it's supposed to be!

The Bible

The local church – imperfect as it often is – is part of that universal church which Christ is building! Jesus declared to Peter in Matthew 16:18-19:

> … I tell you that you are Peter, and on this rock I will build my church, and the gates of Hades will not overcome it. I will give you the keys of the kingdom of heaven; whatever you bind on earth will be bound in heaven, and whatever you loose on earth will be loosed in heaven.

Peter had just professed his faith in Christ. And now he is invited to join Jesus in building something that even hell itself can't overthrow! But please don't miss the point that those who join Peter in this building project are given the authority to declare peoples' sins forgiven or unforgiven based on their response to the gospel! That's a blessing you and I have if we know Christ. We can declare authoritatively—based upon a person's reception or non-reception of the gospel—that their sins have been forgiven and not forgiven. All believers are priests of God and have that God-given authority! We read in 1 Peter 2 verse 9 the following: 'But you are a chosen people, a royal priesthood, a holy nation, God's special possession, that you may declare the praises of him who called you out of darkness into his wonderful light.'

I want to be part of His building project. I want to give my best—my best abilities, resources, time—to what Christ is building. Don't you?

ACTION STEPS

1. Thank the Lord that you as a believer get to do your part in building this hell-conquering project called the church! Text or email someone in leadership in your church this week and express your appreciation for their work.

2. Read Phillip Yancey's short book *Church – Why Bother?* and discuss what you learn from it with another believer.

3. Ask yourself the hard question – How can I more fully support what Jesus is doing in my local church? And am I being trained to do what He wants me to

do? Pray every day this week for wisdom in serving in your local church.

4. PRAYER: Pray for your unsaved friend that he will see that the church is for those in the family of God. The family needs to worship together, serve together, and be together. It may be valuable to have some 'seeker' events in your church to which you can invite your lost friend. Pray that he will see his need of Christ and join the family!

The Blessing of a Longing to Know God

Whatever keeps me from the Bible is my enemy, however harmless it may appear to be. Whatever engages my attention when I should be meditating on God and things eternal does injury to my soul. Let the cares of life crowd out the Scriptures from my mind and I have suffered loss where I can least afford it. Let me accept anything else instead of the Scriptures and I have been cheated and robbed to my eternal confusion (A. W. Tozer).[1]

My friend Mike is unsaved. That's biblical language for his condition before God. In trying to reach my friend, I'm becoming more aware of what I have as a believer and what my friend Mike doesn't yet have.

He believes that he is 'fine' with the Lord. But the critical issue isn't what he thinks, but what God declares. And there is so much more to the Christian life than simply being 'fine' with God. The born-again believer,

---

1. A. W. Tozer, *Gems from Tozer: Selections from the Writings of A. W. Tozer* (Chicago: Moody, 2017) p. 39.

by default, begins a quest of growing deeper in his or her relationship to the Lord.

Let's consider an eighth benefit of the believer which we have and it is that –

WE HAVE A LONGING TO KNOW GOD THROUGH STUDYING HIS WORD!

I heard the story of a professor who was questioned by the police about a student who was being charged with a serious crime. The professor said, 'Oh, yes. He did attend my class. *But he was never my student.*' Some Christians are just 'in the class' and haven't yet realized they are now lifelong *students* of the Word of God!

The Blessing

The believer in Christ has an incredible resource for life in the Word of God, the Bible. He or she can read and study and meditate on the 66 books in the Bible – and be changed in the process!

The Bible

When I became a believer as a teenager, the elders of my church would share a verse with me from the King James Bible: 'Study to shew thyself approved unto God, a workman that needeth not to be ashamed, rightly dividing the word of truth' (2 Tim. 2:15). Their motive was pure. They wanted me to become a *student* of the Word. The word 'study' in this verse is really a word that means 'do your best' or 'be diligent' or 'make every effort.' This same Timothy is commended in 2 Timothy 3 verse 15 with the following words: 'And that from a child thou hast known the holy scriptures, which are able to make thee wise unto salvation through faith which is in Christ Jesus' (KJV). Yes, God's Word can lead one to salvation. But it also inspires a lifelong quest to know the Lord, as the Apostle Paul says in Philippians 3, verse 10, 'That I may know him, and the power of his resurrection, and the fellowship of his sufferings, being made conformable unto his death' (KJV).

When I was in my first year of study at a Bible college, my attitude toward study was, shall we say, severely lacking. If it was a Monday, I'd flip a coin. If it landed heads, I'd play chess with my roommate. If it landed tails, I'd watch Monday night football 'till the wee hours. But if it landed on its edge, I'd study for my classes! The believer in Jesus may not realize it or not, but he or she has enrolled in an eternal class that will never end!

ACTION STEPS

1. Complete the following sentence: 'I want to be a student of God's Word because _____.'

2. Have a conversation with another believer this week who clearly lives to know the Lord better. What are their habits? How do they interact with the Bible on a daily basis? What choices do they make on a daily basis that help them move on in their Christian lives?

3. Read Psalm 63 every day this week and take notes on what it means to long to know the Lord.

4. PRAYER: Pray for your unsaved friend that he would begin to long to know God. Pray for yourself that the two of you would be open to studying the Word together.

⇢ BLESSING 9 ⇠

The Blessing of the Help of the Spirit

> You will find a certain type of preacher and evangelist who claims that he is entirely dependent on the Holy Spirit. It is a blasphemous thing to saddle the Holy Spirit with the blame for rambling, wearisome, and unprepared effusions (William Barclay).[1]

My unsaved friend Mike is helping me become more aware of what I have as a believer and what he doesn't yet have. This list is not given in any sense of gloating, for I grieve for what my friend doesn't yet possess because he isn't yet in God's family.

The Bible is quite clear about the doctrine of the Trinity (even though the word 'trinity' isn't in the Bible). The God who exists is triune – Father, Son, and Holy Spirit. Each is described in Scripture as having various ministries. Let's think about the third member of the Trinity, the One who is often neglected.

---

1. Quoted in Grant R. Osborne and Stephen B. Woodward, *Handbook for Bible Study* (Grand Rapids, MI: Baker, 1979), p. 23.

One of the greatest blessings for the believer is that –

WE HAVE THE SPIRIT OF GOD TO HELP US UNDERSTAND AND APPLY GOD'S WORD!

The Blessing

The third member of the Godhead is personal and divine and we can have a relationship with Him. His deity is made abundantly clear in Acts 5 and His personality (intellect, emotions, and will) is shown in numerous Scriptures (Rom. 8, Acts 13, Eph. 4, Gal. 5, etc.). Although His primary ministry is to direct our attention to Christ and to apply the Word of God to our lives, we can—and should—relate to Him. We are not to grieve Him or quench Him. And we can learn to please Him.

I've written a book (*The Forgotten Third: Developing a Biblical Relationship with God the Holy Spirit*) specifically challenging believers to grow in their connection with the Holy Spirit and to do so by recognizing His ministries in their lives. He is the One who brings conviction of sin (John 16:8-11), bestows spiritual gifts upon God's people (Rom. 12, 1 Cor. 12, Eph. 4, and 1 Pet. 4), reminds us of our place in God's family (Rom. 12), and directs our primary attention to Christ.

One essential ministry of the Spirit of God is that of helping us understand and apply the Word of God to our daily lives.

The Bible

Believers should be dependent on God the Holy Spirit to lead them as they study God's Word. But this is not a substitute for the serious study of the Word, and we are to bring our best hermeneutical skills to the task. The Spirit of God will work with us as we pour over God's truth.

We learn of the Spirit in Jesus' Upper Room Discourse. Jesus says in John 16 – 'But when he, the Spirit of truth, comes, he will guide you into all the truth. He will not speak on his own; he will speak only what he hears, and he will tell you what is yet to come' (v. 13). We also learn in 1 Corinthians 2 that the Spirit of God helps us warmly embrace the truths of God. The unsaved person considers God's Word foolishness and can't understand it because it is discerned only through God's Spirit (vv. 14-15).

ACTION STEPS

1. If the Holy Spirit is divine (and He is), we should worship Him. And if He is personal (and He is), we should talk to Him. Prayer is talking to God. So, write out a prayer to God the Holy Spirit each day this week, asking for His help as you study a passage of Scripture.

2. Sometime this week read J. I. Packer's article on the illumination of the Spirit entitled 'THE HOLY SPIRIT GIVES SPIRITUAL UNDERSTANDING' available through the Monergism website.[2] How is illumination to be understood? What should we say

---

2. J. I. Packer, 'ILLUMINATION: THE HOLY SPIRIT GIVES SPIRITUAL UNDERSTANDING' https://www.monergism.com/ thethreshold/articles/onsite/packer/Illumination.html. This article can also be found in Packer, J. I. *Concise Theology: A Guide to Historic Christian Beliefs* (Carol Stream: Tyndale, 1993), p. 154.

to someone who claims, 'This is what God told me this passage is teaching'?

3. Read my short book, *The Forgotten Third: Developing a Biblical Relationship with God the Holy Spirit.*[3] Discuss what you have learned with another believer.

4. PRAYER: Pray for your lost friend that his heart would be open to the Spirit's work in his life, especially as he reads God's Word. Pray that he would understand— and warmly embrace—the truths of God's Word.

---

3. Larry Dixon, *The Forgotten Third: Developing a Biblical Relationship with God the Holy Spirit* (Gonzalez, Florida: Energion, 2022).

⇀ BLESSING 10 ↽

A Healthy Perspective on Getting Old

You can't help getting older, but you don't have to get old (George Burns).[1]

My friend Mike is helping me become more aware of what I have as a believer and what he doesn't yet have. I'm certainly not gloating, but he inspires me to take stock of what I have in Christ. And what I long for him to have!

My friend is in his eighties. And, like the rest of us, his body is wearing out. He's had two knee replacements and several other surgeries. Each day he gets older (as we all do) and, unless the Lord convicts his heart, closer to being forever separated from God and His love. To me, that is terrifying.

Let's think about a tenth benefit of the believer as we recognize a truth about ourselves and about our unbelieving friends. And it is –

---

1. Lawrence J. Epstein, *George Burns: An American Life* (Jefferson, NC: McFarland Publishing, 2011), p. 174.

WE HAVE A HEALTHY PERSPECTIVE ON GETTING OLD!

If this is the only life one gets, then getting old has got to bring some sadness to the one outside of Christ! Sure, there are joys in seeing one's children grow up, but if in the final analysis one only gets old and dies, that is about as depressing as life can get!

Our culture seems to worship youthfulness. Some cultures seem to honor the aged. What do we learn from the Scriptures about this unavoidable topic?

The Bible

I've recently been going through Psalm 16 with my friend Frank, and there we read in verse 6:

> The boundary lines have fallen for me in pleasant places;
> surely I have a delightful inheritance.

That's what growing older for a believer involves – 'boundary lines' in 'pleasant places'. And for the Christian there is a 'delightful inheritance'! We often think about the inheritance we're going to leave our children and our grandchildren. The psalmist focuses on the inheritance he is going to receive from the Lord!

As one person put it, 'Forget about aging gracefully. Focus instead on aging gratefully.' The believer in Christ can be thankful every day above ground. Each day provides numerous opportunities to serve the Lord, reflect on His goodness, seek to influence others to consider the gospel, grow in one's godliness, etc. For the unbeliever there is only getting older.

In Psalm 21, we read of the godly person, 'He asked you for life, and you gave it to him – length of days, for ever and ever' (v. 4). The believer in Jesus not only has life. He has eternal length of days to worship and serve His Savior. Later, the psalmist writes in this same Psalm, 'Surely you have granted him unending blessings and made him glad with the joy of your presence' (v. 6). That's what the believer in Jesus has – unending blessings! And his gladness is rooted in the joy of God's presence.

My lovely wife recently picked out an emoji (a cartoon picture) to represent herself on the internet. Cute hairstyle, fashionable glasses, adorable face. And she asked me what I thought of her emoji. I said, 'She's very cute – but don't you think you need to add some wrinkles?' I really don't remember much after that. We need to have a biblical view of aging, don't we? I appreciate C. S. Lewis' statement when he said, 'You are never too old to set another goal or to dream a new dream.'

ACTION STEPS

1. Have you thanked the Lord lately for His presence in your getting older? Express to someone today your gratitude for God's sustaining grace in your life. Don't complain about getting older. Praise God—out loud! —for His granting You another day to walk with Him.

2. Have a conversation with someone much older than you in your church one day this week about getting older. What lessons has the Lord taught them over the years about aging? What are some of the 'unending blessings' that they have experienced in walking with the Lord?

3. Psalm 37 has the very famous verse: 'I was young and now I am old, yet I have never seen the righteous forsaken or their children begging bread' (v. 25). Read over this Psalm every day this week and ask what lessons there are in this Psalm about being 'old' in the Lord.

4. PRAYER: How do I pray for my unsaved friend? I can pray that he would see his days and months and years as a gift from God and that he would turn to the Lord for salvation! Eternity – not nothingness – awaits. And we can use our time here for honoring Him!

⇝ BLESSING 11 ⇜

The Blessing of a Defendable Worldview

The Dalai Lama, the spiritual leader of the Tibetan people, has said, 'This is my simple religion. There is no need for temples; no need for complicated philosophy. Our own brain, our own heart is our temple; the philosophy is kindness.'[1]

God's Word is filled with blessings that belong only to the saved. My friend Mike is lost and, therefore, doesn't enjoy any of these benefits. Do I? Am I aware of all that I have 'in Christ'?

In thinking about the many blessings which our unsaved friends don't have, we need to think about another blessing which we followers of Christ have been given and it is this –

WE HAVE A DEFENDABLE WORLDVIEW!

The Blessing

Not to get too philosophical, but any worldview other than that given by God in His Word is susceptible to

---

1. Aksapāda, *1400 Lessons from the 14th Dalai Lama* (Kindle Edition. Published February 26, 2019), p. 49.

attack and eventual overthrow. Wow! What a dogmatic statement! But, seriously, if biblical Christianity isn't true and the Bible isn't God's Word, why should we bother following Christ? There are clear and strong evidences of the Bible's truthfulness; Christ's life, death, burial, and resurrection; and the fact that the God of the Bible is real and holy and angry at sin.

Because biblical Christianity is an organized system of truth, we can set forth evidence, examine alternatives, and draw reasonable conclusions about the most critical issues in life. Contrary to what the Dalai Lama says, we are not our own gods. The God of the Bible stands outside us, is independent of us, and has broken into His creation through the person of Jesus Christ.

Biblical Christianity answers the most important questions of life. What is the meaning of life? What do I do with my sense of guilt? Have I really been made in the image and likeness of a personal God? What is God like? How can I have a relationship with Him? Is the Bible really God's Word – and can I trust it? These and other critical questions are given sufficient answers in biblical Christianity.

The Bible

The Bible presents many examples of believers defending the truth of the gospel. Acts 17 is a great illustration of a philosophically-informed Apostle Paul presenting the truth about Jesus. In fact, he presents the gospel with five different groups of unbelievers using pagan literature as his contact point.

Jesus' followers are commanded to be ready to give reasons for their faith in their Savior. We read in 1 Peter 3:15:

> But in your hearts revere Christ as Lord. Always be prepared to give an answer to everyone who asks you to give the reason for the hope that you have. But do this with gentleness and respect…

Please notice in this passage that the defense of our faith (1) begins in our hearts! We revere, show proper respect for, the Lord, when we are ready to stand up for the truth. Notice also that (2) we are to always be prepared to give an answer. Preparation takes effort and study and intention. Notice as well that (3) we should expect people to ask us about our faith! It's a lot easier to witness when we are asked about our walk with the Lord. And, lastly, this passage teaches that (4) our attitude (gentleness and respect) are really important to our witness.

ACTION STEPS

1. Our society suffers from what one writer calls 'truth decay.' Another has said that 'Apart from blunt truth, our lives sink decadently amid the perfume of hints and suggestions.' Study at least ten verses on truth (perhaps two per day) that you find in the Scriptures. How might you practically stand for the truth of the gospel?

2. If you've been a believer for a while, become friends with someone from a different religion or even a cult. Ask them a lot of questions about their faith

and graciously share with them what you know about Jesus' identity and His being the only way to salvation.

3. Consider offering a group study on a book like *Mere Christianity* by C. S. Lewis. And make sure some participants aren't yet believers!

4. PRAYER How do I pray for my unsaved friend? First, I need to understand his present worldview. Second, I need to do whatever I can to challenge it in light of the gospel. And, third, I need to pray for God the Holy Spirit to open my friend's eyes to how he ought to view life and eternity and ... Jesus.

⇢ BLESSING 12 ⇠

The Blessing of a Permanent Joy

Joseph Haydn was once criticized for the gaiety of his church music. He replied: 'I cannot help it. I give forth what is in me. When I think of the Divine Being, my heart is so full of joy that the notes fly off as from a spindle. And as I have a cheerful heart, He will pardon me if I serve Him cheerfully.'[1]

'Count your blessings – Name them one by one …' I sang this song as a young Christian. In thinking about my unsaved friend Mike, I'm counting the blessings I have in Christ. My heart goes out to him – for he doesn't have these blessings because he doesn't have the Lord.

I long for my friend to have this next blessing. And I want to remind my family in Christ that –

WE HAVE A PERMANENT JOY!

The Blessing

My friend Mike seems to be a happy person. He is outgoing, generous, and kind. I imagine he would describe himself as a relatively happy individual.

---

1. Quoted in Emil Naumann and F. A. Gore Ouseley, *The History of Music: Volume 2* (Palala Press, 2016), p. 879.

But joy is quite different from the kind of temporary happiness our world offers. Happiness, as someone has said, depends on *happenings*. Joy in Christ is not dependent on what takes place in our world – or in our lives.

Joy for the believer is solid and lasting and eternal, for it comes from the everlasting God! Dr. Willard S. Krabill has said that 'The mentally and emotionally healthy are those that have learned when to say Yes, when to say No, and when to say Whoopee!'[2]

The Bible

Jesus had much to say about joy. He promises a complete joy in John 15:11 when He says, 'I have told you this so that my joy may be in you and that your joy may be complete.' He challenges His followers in John 16 by saying, 'Until now you have not asked for anything in my name. Ask and you will receive, and your joy will be complete.' (v. 24). I wonder how many of Jesus' followers are living with an incomplete joy? Perhaps an incomplete joy may be defined as a joy that does not center on the Lord Jesus and all He has done for us. Jesus also promises that the disciples' grief will turn to joy in John 16:20 and He assures His followers that no one can take away their joy (v. 22).

Spiritual leaders like C. S. Lewis and John Piper focused much of their ministry on the concept of pursuing joy in the Lord. 'Joy is the serious business of heaven,' Lewis said. He also wrote,

---

2. Quoted in Frank B. Minirth and Mark Littleton, *You Can! Seven Principles for Winning in Life* (Nashville, TN: Thomas Nelson, 1994), p. 104.

Either the day must come when joy prevails and all the makers of misery are no longer able to infect it, or else, for ever and ever, the makers of misery can destroy in others the happiness they reject for themselves.[3]

Pastor John Piper so aptly wrote,

Christ did not die to forgive sinners who go on treasuring anything above seeing and savoring God. And people who would be happy in heaven if Christ were not there, will not be there. The gospel is not a way to get people to heaven; it is a way to get people to God. It's a way of overcoming every obstacle to everlasting joy in God. If we don't want God above all things, we have not been converted by the gospel.[4]

ACTION STEPS

1. List several joy killers that you have experienced recently. These may be circumstances – or people! What steps can you take to not allow those issues or individuals to steal your joy?

2. Unit-reading is reading an entire book of the Bible at one sitting. Unit-read the book of Philippians each day this week, and take a few notes on the topic of joy.

3. 'The joyful Christian is an arresting advertisement of the gospel,' someone once said. We all have different personalities. Would your friends and associates describe you as a joyful person? Why or why not?

---

3. C. S. Lewis, *The Complete C. S. Lewis Signature Classics* (New York City: HarperCollins, 2016), p. 536.

4. John Piper, *God Is the Gospel: Meditations on God's Love as the Gift of Himself* (Wheaton: Crossway, 2011), p. 47.

4. PRAYER How do I pray for my unsaved friend? First, I need to show that joy in Jesus that my friend does not yet have. Second, I need to pray that he would sense a lack of true, biblical joy in his life.

⇢ BLESSING 13 ⇠

The Blessing of a Proper Fear

I may tremble on the Rock, but the Rock never trembles under me! And that inner assurance not only relieves my fear, it allows me to carry on with much greater efficiency. And rather than causing me to be indifferent and irresponsible, it inspires me to direct all my energies toward those things that please and glorify the name of my heavenly Father ... eternally protected because He has me in His all-powerful hand (Chuck Swindoll).[1]

As we continue to 'count our blessings,' there is one which we seldom think about. We live in a culture which thinks that almost all fear is bad, especially a fear of God. However, as we engage with our lost friends who don't have this particular blessing, we believers –

WE HAVE A PROPER FEAR!

The Blessing

There is both proper and improper fear. Running out of a cabin in Arizona when you hear a rattling sound makes

---

1. Charles R. Swindoll, *Stress Fractures: Advice and Encouragement for Handling Your Face-Paced Life* (Grand Rapids: Zondervan, 1992), p. 129.

perfect sense, unless you enjoy an up-close and personal encounter with a rattlesnake! Some fears are groundless; many are life-saving.

The Bible

But what about a fear of GOD? Many in our culture habitually use God's name as a curse word, mock those who believe in Jesus, and think there will be no judgment day. The Bible declares such to be *fools*! As one preacher put it, 'You will stand before God's judgment whether you think you will or not.'

We read that 'the fear of the Lord is the beginning of wisdom' (Ps. 111:10) and that 'The fear of the Lord is pure, enduring forever' (Ps. 19:9). We are told, 'How abundant are the good things that you have stored up for those who fear you, that you bestow in the sight of all, on those who take refuge in you' (Ps. 31:19). There is no better place in which we can find refuge than in the God who saved us by His Son's sacrifice. We are challenged in Psalm 34 that we should 'Fear the LORD, you his holy people, for those who fear him lack nothing' (v. 9). *And the above verses are from only one book of the Bible!*

We read in the New Testament that 'It is a dreadful thing to fall into the hands of the living God' (Heb. 10:31). Two chapters later we read, 'Therefore, since we are receiving a kingdom that cannot be shaken, let us be thankful, and so worship God acceptably with reverence and awe, for our "God is a consuming fire"'(12:28-29).

C. S. Lewis put it this way:

God is the only comfort, He is also the supreme terror: the thing we most need and the thing we most want to hide from. He is our only possible ally, and we have made ourselves His enemies. Some people talk as if meeting the gaze of absolute goodness would be fun. They need to think again. They are still only playing with religion. Goodness is either the great safety or the great danger – according to the way you react to it. And we have reacted the wrong way.[2]

ACTION STEPS

1. What other verses in Scripture can you find which describe biblical fear? Write out one verse each day which shows that a biblical fear is a good thing.

2. Read Jonathan Edwards' sermon 'Sinners in the Hands of an Angry God' (found online) this week. Don't allow your high school English teacher's criticism of that sermon deter you from its primary challenge. How does Edwards use the concept of fear to reach the lost?

3. Perhaps ask your unsaved friend, 'What are you most afraid of?' Seek, by God's wisdom, why they do not fear standing before a holy God at the end of life.

4. PRAYER How do I pray for my unsaved friend? I pray to God the Holy Spirit that my friend would think about the holiness of God and his own need of forgiveness, that somehow he would realize that 'it is a fearful thing to fall into the hands of the living God' (Heb. 10:31 KJV), that the Spirit of God would bring conviction of sin to his soul.

2. Lyle W. Dorsett (Editor), *The Essential C. S. Lewis*. Edited and with an Introduction (New York: Scribner, 1988), p. 311.

The Blessing of a Balanced Emotional Life

This quote bears repeating: 'The mentally and emotionally healthy are those that have learned when to say Yes, when to say No, and when to say Whoopee!' (Dr. Willard S. Krabill).

I believe we should *rejoice* in the many blessings we have as followers of Jesus. And, conversely, I think we should *grieve* for those we love who don't yet know Christ – and, therefore, don't have these blessings. Grieving and rejoicing are emotions – and emotions are critical for human life.

However, what emotions should mark the follower of Jesus? And how do we know when our emotions are appropriate? Sometimes I get really happy about things that don't matter all that much. I also find that a lot of times I'm not concerned about the things that truly count. How can I know how I'm supposed to feel?

The emotional life of the believer is very important. God made us with emotions, but, like the other aspects of our personality, our emotions are fallen, twisted, out of balance, frequently inappropriate. So I would suggest that one of our blessings in being saved is –

WE CAN HAVE BALANCED EMOTIONS!

The Blessing

'Balanced' might not be the right word. But I believe that knowing Christ fundamentally renews and re-orients all that we are (our intellect, will, and emotions). I need to weep over what grieves the heart of God and rejoice in those truths that He has graciously given in His Word and in His world.

The Bible

Some would suggest that one can't help how one feels. But certain emotions and thoughts are clearly described in Scripture as sin. For example, if a man looks at a woman with lust in his heart, Jesus says, that he has *already* committed adultery (Matt. 5:28)! This issue of committing adultery in one's heart is so serious that Jesus advises gouging out one's eye or cutting off one's right hand to avoid such a sin (vv. 29-30)!

Lest we think that our emotions only get us into sin, we are reminded that we are to be joyful in tribulation (Heb. 10:34), hateful of sin (Amos 5:15), and burdened for those who are struggling with sin (Gal. 6:2).

Jesus was not just a man of sorrows. He was also a man of JOY. He says to His disciples in John 15, 'These things have I spoken unto you, that my joy might remain in you, and that your joy might be full' (v. 11 KJV). One of the most important things a Christian can do is to study the emotional life of the Lord Jesus. What brought Him sadness? Disappointment? Excitement? Regret? Joy?

The Bible puts a premium on our proper emotions. Psalm 126 refers to 'Those who go out *weeping*, carrying seed to sow, will return with songs of *joy*, carrying sheaves with them' (v. 6). And the believer is clearly commanded in Romans 12:15 to '*Rejoice* with those who *rejoice*; *mourn* with those who *mourn*.'

ACTION STEPS

1. Someone has said that the only thing Job's friends did that was right was that they sat with him on the ground silent for seven days and seven nights, weeping. This week, find someone who is weeping and weep with them. We are to rejoice with those who rejoice. Find someone this week who is rejoicing – and join them!

2. The Lord Jesus is to be our model in all aspects of life. This week, read through one of the gospels and underline every emotion you see in the life and ministry of the Lord Jesus. What are some practical lessons you are learning as you do that study?

3. You might consider reading the classic book by James Dobson entitled *Emotions: Can You Trust Them?* Discuss the book with a friend.

4. PRAYER So, how do I pray for my unsaved friend? I show by my godly emotions both appropriate joy and grief in life. I rejoice in God's blessing of him and am concerned about the things that trouble him. And I

pray for my friend that the Holy Spirit would give him a longing to know God personally and rejoice eternally in Him!

→ BLESSING 15 ←

The Blessing of a Godly Hatred

I will tell you what to hate. Hate hypocrisy, hate can't, hate indolence, oppression, injustice; hate Pharisaism; hate them as Christ hated them – with a deep, living, Godlike hatred (Frederick William Robertson).[1]

We believers in Jesus are so blessed! Do we realize all the benefits of being saved, being made right with the Lord? My unsaved friend Mike doesn't. Yet. So I'm counting some of my blessings as I think about what Mike doesn't have as an unbeliever.

One of the most surprising truths about biblical Christianity is the fact that there is both godly and ungodly jealously, godly and ungodly pride, and godly and ungodly *hatred*. Really!

Our culture so emphasizes love that it doesn't realize there is a place for biblical hatred! For believers it might be said that –

WE POSSESS A GODLY HATRED!

---

1. Frederick William Robertson, *Sermons Preached at Brighton* (New York: Harper & Brothers, 1873). Np.

The Blessing

We should hate hypocrisy, despise pedophilia, abhor child abuse, absolutely renounce racism, right? There is both godly and ungodly hatred. The actor Will Smith once said, 'Throughout life people will make you mad, disrespect you and treat you bad. Let God deal with the things they do, cause hate in your heart will consume you too.'[2] The challenge is to turn away from ungodly hatred and to embrace a godly revulsion toward those things He hates.

The Bible

It is quite surprising to see what the Bible has to say about God hating and also how believers are to hate. Here are some representative verses of God hating:

1. 'The arrogant cannot stand in your presence. You hate all who do wrong' (Ps. 5:5).

2. 'The Lord examines the righteous, but the wicked, those who love violence, he hates with a passion' (Ps. 11:5).

3. 'Your New Moon feasts and your appointed festivals I hate with all my being' (Isa. 1:14).

4. 'Because of all their wickedness in Gilgal, I hated them there' (Hosea 9:15).

5. '"Do not plot evil against each other, and do not love to swear falsely. I hate all this," declares the Lord' (Zech. 8:17).

---

2. Part of this quotation comes from Will Smith's song 'Just the Two of Us,' but the quotation as is circulates regularly around the internet and is quoted in many books and interviews. https://www.letssingit.com/will-smith-lyrics-just-the-two-of-us-3d8s363

6. '... I have loved Jacob, but Esau I have hated' (Mal. 1:2-3).

One might make the point that a few of these texts sound like hyperbole, but not all of them. What verses do we have that say the child of God is to hate?

1. We read that there is 'a time to love and a time to hate' (Eccles. 3:8).

2. The psalmist says, 'I hate those who cling to worthless idols; as for me, I trust in the LORD.' (Ps. 31:6).

3. Psalm 97 commands, 'Let those who love the LORD hate evil' (v. 10).

4. Amos 5:15 issues the challenge: 'Hate evil, love good; maintain justice in the courts.'

5. Jesus speaks about hatred in both Luke 14:26 and John 12:25 where we read, 'If anyone comes to me and does not hate father and mother, wife and children, brothers and sisters—yes, even their own life—such a person cannot be my disciple.' John 12:25 says, 'Anyone who loves their life will lose it, while anyone who hates their life in this world will keep it for eternal life.'

6. The Apostle Paul uses strong language as he thinks about his behavior as a believer: 'I do not understand what I do. For what I want to do I do not do, but what I hate I do' (Rom. 7:15).

7. Paul seems to be referring back to the Amos passage when he says in Romans 12, 'Love must be sincere. Hate what is evil; cling to what is good' (v. 9).

8. The Apostle John quotes the Lord in Revelation 2 saying of the Ephesian church, '… you have this in your favor: You hate the practices of the Nicolaitans, which I also hate' (v. 6).

We might not like what the Bible says in those verses, but there it is. We are to reject and hate evil in our world – and in ourselves. Believers must define and defend biblical hatred even as they love those for whom Christ died.

ACTION STEPS

1. Imagine that your unsaved friend says to you, 'I hear that Christians are to *hate?* That can't be right!' How would you answer your friend using some of the verses above?

2. Think about Proverbs 6:16 ('There are six things the LORD hates …') and list one practical way every day this week that you can show your hatred of the things God hates.

3. Read Tim Challies' article on God's hatred[3] and answer the question, 'Why does God hate idolatry so much?'

4. PRAYER So, how do I pray for my unsaved friend? I show by my godly life that I am grieved and angered at the effects of evil in our world and seek to do whatever I can to be salt and light in my culture. And I pray for my lost friend that he would experience a proper self-hatred that drives him to the Savior.

---

3. https://www.challies.com/articles/hate-what-god-hates/

⤜ BLESSING 16 ⤛

The Blessing of a Reason to Sing

I always try to cheer myself up by singing when I get sad. Most of the time, it turns out that my voice is worse than my problems (anonymous).[1]

Almost each Saturday I'm given a 'honey-do' list. These are jobs my wife of fifty years wants me to complete. Lists are important, aren't they? If you had to make a list of the blessings you have as a believer, what would your list look like? Would it be just a few items? Or would you need a second or a third page?

My friend Mike—who has not yet trusted Christ as his Savior—enjoys many of the common grace blessings of a providential God, but is missing out on so many benefits of being in the family of God. I've recently been listening to some powerful Christian music (I'm a Lauren Daigle fan) and it dawned on me that those who belong to the Lord –

---

1. This anonymous quotation circulates on social media, but no author is ever given nor original source of the quotation.

WE HAVE A REASON TO SING!

Of course, those who don't know Christ have their music. The outright skeptic Friedrich Nietzsche said, 'Without music, life would be a mistake.'[2] Some of the world's music is quite good. But heartfelt praise to God for all He has done for them? That's a tune they have yet to learn.

The Bible

I love the quote which says, 'Singing in the shower is all fun and games until you get shampoo in your mouth. Then it becomes a soap opera!' Music, singing, dancing are very important in the Scriptures. Psalm 96:1-3 says,

> Sing to the LORD a new song; sing to the LORD, all the earth. Sing to the LORD, praise his name; proclaim his salvation day after day. Declare his glory among the nations, his marvelous deeds among all peoples.

2 Samuel 22 says, 'Therefore I will praise you, LORD, among the nations; I will sing the praises of your name' (v. 50). 1 Chronicles challenges the believer to 'Sing to him, sing praise to him; tell of all his wonderful acts' (16:9). And the writer gets even more specific about the theme of our singing later in the same chapter: 'Sing to the LORD, all the earth; proclaim his *salvation* day after day' (v. 23).

You see, the problem with my friend is that he hasn't become convinced that he is in grave danger without Christ. The psalmist hits this note when he writes, 'But

---

2. Michael Feinstein, *The Gershwins and Me (Enhanced Edition): A Personal History in Twelve Songs* (New York: Simon & Schuster, 2012), p. 228.

let all who take refuge in you be glad; let them ever sing for joy. Spread your protection over them, that those who love your name may rejoice in you' (Ps. 5:11). This same idea of finding refuge in the Lord is reiterated in Psalm 59: 'But I will sing of your strength, in the morning I will sing of your love; for you are my fortress, my refuge in times of trouble' (v. 16).

The believer in Christ recognizes the many blessings of being in Christ: 'I will sing the LORD's praise, for he has been good to me' (Ps. 13:6). And the psalmist invites us to 'Sing to him a new song; play skillfully, and shout for joy' (Ps. 33:3).

ACTION STEPS

1. Someone has said that music is 'unfrozen theology.' That is, we sing what we believe. Take a few minutes this week and analyze one of the songs you sang in church on Sunday. What theology (doctrine) did it celebrate?

2. The Psalms were written to be sung. In fact, some of them have at the beginning words like 'to be sung to the tune of …' Select one Psalm each day this week and experiment by singing each to the Lord with your own tune!

3. Read over Matthew 26:20-30 each day this week. Notice that Jesus and His disciples sang a hymn together (v. 30). We don't know what that hymn was, but imagine you were with the Lord. What might you have heard?

4. PRAYER So, how do I pray for my unsaved friend? First of all, he needs to hear me sing (figuratively if not literally)! He needs to see a tangible joy in my life that can't keep me from bursting into song. And, second, I need to pray that God the Holy Spirit would bring that new song to his heart.

The Blessing of a Prayer Life

Samuel Chadwick, one of the greatest preachers of English Methodism, once said, 'The one concern of the devil is to keep God's people from praying ... He laughs at your toil and he mocks at your wisdom. But he *trembles* when you pray!'[1]

My lost friend Mike drives me to my knees every day as I think about what he *doesn't* have in not knowing Christ. And his lack helps me focus on my blessings so I can pray for him to come into God's family.

We are commanded in Psalm 103 to 'Praise the LORD, my soul, and forget not all his benefits ...' (v. 2). I don't think most Christians even *know* all the benefits they have in being saved. It's hard to forget what we aren't aware we have.

Let's think about another benefit or blessing which followers of Jesus have –

WE HAVE A PRAYER LIFE!

1. *The New Encyclopedia of Christian Quotations* (Hampshire, UK: John Hunt Publishing, 2000), p. 783.

I am not suggesting that my lost friends never pray. I'm sure many of them do. They pray when a loved one is seriously ill, when they've lost a job, when a child has wandered from the family at the beach and gotten lost, when the doctor comes in and says, 'I'm sorry. But I have bad news.' And we Christians pray the same SOS prayers, don't we?

The Blessing

But I'm thinking about a prayer LIFE. What do I mean? I mean the believer should treat prayer as a critical weapon in his arsenal. He resorts to prayer when under attack by his supernatural foe, the devil. He turns to the Lord in faith when all around him seems to shout, 'you've been abandoned by your God!' He cries out to the Father when he faces situations he hasn't been able to deal with on his own.

The Bible

But those circumstances are emergency situations. How about daily interceding for our loved ones, praying for another believer's spiritual growth, pleading with the Lord for a friend's salvation? The prophet Samuel hit the nail on the head when he said to the people of Israel: 'As for me, far be it from me that I should sin against the LORD by failing to pray for you' (1 Sam. 12:23). Do we believers ever think of our failure to pray for others as *a sin against the Lord?!*

And we need to pray for ourselves. For we have many needs – that the Lord would reorder our priorities (Eph. 5:17); that He would give us His joy when life brings us down (John 15:11); that we would rely on His strength instead of our own (Ps. 20:7); that we would engage in precious times of contemplating the Lord and His attributes (His mercy, goodness, kindness, strength, love, etc.; Pss. 1:2; 77:12; 119:148; 143:5; 1 Tim. 4:15). How we must grieve the heart of God when we treat Him only as a kind of celestial vending machine. He is our Father, our Lord, our best friend, our Savior.

Scripture teaches us that prayer – (1) Can keep us from falling into temptation (Matt. 26:41); (2) Can help us love our enemies (Matt. 6:5); (3) Can give us sweet and secret times with our Father (Matt. 6:6); (4) Can remind us of God's knowledge of our circumstances (Matt. 6:9); (5) Can test our belief in God's meeting our needs (Matt. 21:22); (6) Can clarify God's will for us and for others (Rom. 1:10); (7) Can make us aware of the Spirit's assistance in interceding for us (Rom. 8:26); (8) Can test our faithfulness (Rom. 12:12); (9) Can practically help other believers (2 Cor. 1:11); (10) Can motivate us to pray for the spiritual growth of others (Eph. 1:18); etc.

ACTION STEPS

1. Thank God for the gift of prayer, confessing your poor exercise of that discipline, if such is the case.

2. Is it not true that we often pray only mundane (meaning 'earthly') prayers, for such matters as health and jobs and conflicts? Each day this week read over one of the Apostle Paul's prayers for a co-worker (such as Col. 1:9-14) and make a list of what Paul prays for, for others. Do the same for one of your friends each day this week.

3. Begin a prayer journal. This need not require a massive amount of time and energy, but make a few daily notes on what are the top items on your prayer list.

4. PRAYER Pray for your unsaved friend – and perhaps even let him know that you are praying for him. Agree to pray for whatever he requests, and keep some notes so you can update your prayers for him.

✣ BLESSING 18 ✣

The Blessing of a Plan for Intentional Parenting

If it weren't for families, we'd have to fight with strangers!
(Anonymous).

There are so many blessings in knowing Christ, right?
Not just salvation. As I pray for and reflect on my
friendship with Mike, I'm becoming more aware of what
I have in knowing Christ. And I wish the same for every
believer!

It bugs me that many Christians don't understand
the multi-faceted instruction book that they have in the
Bible, God's Word! Scripture not only tells how to get
saved, but how to *live*. And one major area of life is ...
parenting.

The Blessing
Many Christian parents, I would suggest, haven't really
dug into the Bible to see what it says about being a godly
husband, a loving wife, obedient and joyful children, etc.
So I would remind Jesus' followers that –

WE HAVE A PLAN FOR INTENTIONAL PARENTING!

Some of my unsaved friends appear to be great fathers and mothers. But, can we talk? That's only because they are *borrowing* parenting skills from Christianity – and probably don't even know it. Others of my friends aren't loving their spouses as they should, are allowing their children to have whatever they want, whenever they want it, and seem to be investing zero minutes in training their children in godliness.

The Bible

Such must not be the family situation of the follower of Jesus. The Bible gives us clear guidance on: (1) being a godly husband (Eph. 5:23-33; Titus 1:6); (2) being a loving and supportive wife (Eph. 5:22); and (3) having obedient, believing children (Titus 1:6; 1 Tim. 3:4). God's Word provides us clear instructions on caring for the elderly (Lev. 19:32; 1 Tim. 5:1; 1 Pet. 5:5; Isa. 46:4) and widows (1 Tim. 5). Sadly, Scripture presents us with case studies of families that fell apart. But we have also the encouraging story of Job who sacrificed and prayed daily for his children. We read the following in Job 1:1-5:

> In the land of Uz there lived a man whose name was Job. This man was blameless and upright; he feared God and shunned evil. He had seven sons and three daughters, and he owned seven thousand sheep, three thousand camels, five hundred yoke of oxen and five hundred donkeys, and had a large number of servants. He was the greatest man among all the people of the East.

His sons used to hold feasts in their homes on their birthdays, and they would invite their three sisters to eat and drink with them. When a period of feasting had run its course, Job would make arrangements for them to be purified. Early in the morning he would sacrifice a burnt offering for each of them, thinking, 'Perhaps my children have sinned and cursed God in their hearts.' This was Job's regular custom.

What is the 'regular custom' of us fathers in the 21st Century? This first chapter of Job makes it clear that the trials through which God is going to put Job are not because of his sin (he was 'blameless and upright; he feared God and shunned evil'). His life will be sorely tested, especially by his friends who try in vain to bring him to his senses. But daily, Job sacrificed for each of his ten children *just in case* they had sinned and cursed God in their hearts!

One of my unsaved friends is making some poor choices in his family. He loves his daughter much more than his wife. He doesn't feel he is respected by either. He simply doesn't have the foundation to be the spiritual leader in his family. And, sadly, I don't think their marriage is going to make it.

However, good news! This friend is actually thinking about having a Bible study with me on the gospel of John! Pray that he will come to Christ and become the husband and father God wants him to be.

ACTION STEPS

1. Pick one set of Scriptures listed above ('The Bible gives us clear guidance on ...') and write out an action plan

of obeying what God's Word says. Share your plan with another believer this week who can pray for you and ask you how you are doing.

2. Invite a couple from your church (whose family you admire) for lunch and interview them sometime this week on what practices have been most helpful to them in their family.

3. Read a book like Dennis & Barbara Rainey's *Growing a Spiritually Strong Family* with your spouse and pray together about what you learn.

4. PRAYER Take steps to open your home to your unsaved friends so they can observe some of what you intentionally practice in your family. Invite them to a game night or a movie night.

⤞ BLESSING 19 ⤝

The Blessing of a Proper View of Health

Happiness is nothing more than good health and a bad memory (Albert Schweitzer).[1]

In his book *God Is the Gospel* Pastor John Piper makes the basic point that 'When you trusted Christ, you got God!' Absolutely. But what else did we 'get' when we believed the gospel?

My friend Mike is as lost as lost can be (as I was before Jesus saved me). And he has got me thinking about all that I have as a believer. So I'm making a list...

Our culture, it seems, is health-obsessed. Vitamins, exercise machines, weight loss programs, skinny Photoshopped models, plastic surgery, diets and diet pills, and multiple over-the-counter and prescription drugs all scream messages at us: 'HEALTH! You must be healthy!

---

1. Joachim Weimann, Andreas Knabe and Ronnie Schöb, *Measuring Happiness: The Economics of Well-Being* (Cambridge, MA: The MIT Press, 2015), p. 41.

Here's a pill for this problem! Join this weight-loss plan right now! You don't have to suffer with the heartbreak of psoriasis!'

Please don't misunderstand me. I'm grateful for advances in medicine, programs that help me live longer, and practical steps I can take to be healthier. I just wonder if we're more focused on better health than we ought to be. Has it become for some an idol? For that reason, I believe that we Christians –

HAVE A PROPER VIEW OF HEALTH!

The Blessing

Of course we should make healthy choices in what we eat, how much we exercise, how we treat the one body God has given us for this life. But, for some, perfect health has become their god. Believers in Jesus recognize that they are stewards or managers of the one life God has entrusted to them.

You may have heard the story of the bride who when asked, 'Do you take this man for better, for worse, for richer, for poorer, in sickness and in health, to love and cherish, until we are parted by death?' responded: 'Yes, No, Yes, No, No, Yes'!

Jesus' followers are to serve Him in sickness and in health. Prosperity theology which says believers should always be healthy and wealthy misses this commitment to Christ.

The Bible

What, then, would be a biblical view of health? Several principles occur to me: (1) We should acknowledge that our bodies are given to us by God (Gen. 2:7, 18-25); (2) we should agree that our bodies are not our own (1 Cor. 3:16-17 and 6); (3) we should take care of the physical part of who we are (Eph. 5:28-29); (4) we should honor God even in our 'disabilities' ('Who gave human beings their mouths? Who makes them deaf or mute? Who gives them sight or makes them blind? Is it not I, the LORD?' (Exod. 4:11); (5) we should seek healing if such is God's will (James 5:14); and (6) we should honor the Lord even in our infirmities (2 Cor. 12).

Prosperity theology is one-dimensional. Sometimes, the Lord sends affliction into our lives for His purposes. And we can sometimes honor Him best, not through our health, but in our brokenness.

ACTION STEPS

1. We believers need to model a balanced view of health, avoiding either the extreme of neglect or the worship of our bodies. We believe that matter *matters*, that God made our bodies, and we should be good stewards of our physical beings. List one practical step that you can take each day this week to live a healthier life.

2. We read in Romans 12:1-2 the following –

   Therefore, I urge you, brothers and sisters, in view of God's mercy, to offer your bodies as a living sacrifice, holy and pleasing to God – this is your true and proper worship. Do not conform to the pattern of this world, but be transformed by the renewing of your mind. Then you will be able to test and approve what God's will is – his good, pleasing and perfect will.

This passage makes several critical statements about our bodies. Read those verses in a different version of the Bible each day this week and write out several implications for your health and fitness.

3. I have been greatly helped on this issue of matter mattering to God by reading Michael Witmer's book *Becoming Worldly Saints: Can You Serve Jesus and Still Enjoy Your Life?* Consider reading that book along with a friend and discussing it.

4. PRAYER Sometimes, unbelievers think we Christians care only about the spiritual. Share with your friend some of your concern about your physical health and how our bodies matter to the Lord.

The Blessing of a Biblical Perspective on Risk

There is a warning. The path of God-exalting joy will cost you your life. ... [I]t is better to lose your life than to waste it. If you live gladly to make others glad in God, your life will be hard, your risks will be high, and your joy will be full. ... Some of you will die in the service of Christ. That will not be a tragedy. Treasuring life above Christ is a tragedy (John Piper).[1]

If your lost friend were to ask you, 'What's the best part about being a follower of Jesus?', what would you say? Of course, salvation would be the first answer most of us would give. But what might be the second or third matter you would state? What are some of *the other blessings* you enjoy which your unsaved friend doesn't have? Yet.

One blessing that perhaps doesn't occur to a lot of us is that of *being able to take risks for the kingdom of God.* As followers of Jesus –

---

1. John Piper, *Don't Waste Your Life* (Wheaton, IL: Crossway, 2018), p. 10.

WE HAVE A BIBLICAL PERSPECTIVE ON RISK!

Life *is* risky, isn't it? We're not to live foolishly, but living a totally risk-free life is impossible. At any moment in our lives we might become the victim of a crime, be overcome by an unexpected disease, or be mistreated by our godless culture. These outside forces often pose great and unavoidable risks to us.

The Blessing

But *can we put ourselves at risk*? Should we? In his book *Risk Is Right*, Pastor John Piper makes the critical point that it is better to lose your life than to waste it! Here are some risks that a believer is free to make: Sharing the gospel and being rejected by one's friends. Serving the Lord in far-flung places in the world where people eat what people were never intended to eat! Standing for truth at the cost of a promotion or the possibility of being sued! Being faithful in one's marriage even when one's spouse has bailed out of their wedding vows. Such worthwhile risks the unbeliever knows little to nothing about.

The Bible

People in the Bible were constantly at risk. David frequently cries out to the Lord to save him from those who want him dead. The early Christians laid down their lives for the gospel – and thought such to be a privilege! Acts 15:26 speaks of 'men who have risked their lives for the name of our Lord Jesus Christ.' Paul calls Priscilla and Aquila 'my co-workers in Christ Jesus [who] risked their lives for me' (Rom. 16:3-4). In Philippians 2:26-30, Epaphroditus is described as one who

> longs for all of you and is distressed because you heard he was ill ... and almost died. But God had mercy on him ... Therefore I am all the more eager to send him, so that when you see him again you may be glad and I may have less anxiety. So then, welcome him in the Lord with great joy, and honor people like him, because he almost died for the work of Christ. He risked his life to make up for the help you yourselves could not give me.

We may pray like the psalmist in Psalm 16, 'Keep me safe, my God, for in you I take refuge' (v. 1). It's not wrong to ask God to keep us safe, but not risk-free! We believers know that this life is not the only one there is, and we might well lose our lives for the gospel. The unbeliever does not have this 'blessing.'

ACTION STEPS

1. Ask yourself the question, 'What risks am I willing to take for the gospel?' I may need to begin by apologizing to my family or friends for failing to live as I should before them. Take one risk this week which you know will glorify the Lord. And share your experience with another believer.

2. Interview a missionary this week who is serving the Lord in a dangerous place. Ask him or her about this issue of risk. Commit yourself to pray for them and their safety as they risk their lives for the gospel.

3. Read Piper's short book *Risk Is Right*. Take notes on your reading and discuss the book with a Christian friend or two.

4. PRAYER Pray that your lost friend will understand that the highest goal in life should not be one's physical or emotional survival. Treasuring Christ is far more critical.

→ BLESSING 21 ←

The Blessing of Future Rewards

Don't try to get all your rewards on earth. There are more rewards in Heaven (Bo Sanchez).[1]

I have a friend who does my taxes. It's not that I'm not good with numbers, but with our small Amazon business, I need help figuring out my assets and my liabilities. In this study we're thinking about our blessings, our spiritual assets, as it were. And I'm inspired to think about this list because of my unsaved friend Mike who doesn't yet enjoy these blessings.

Of the righteous person, the psalmist says, 'Surely you have granted him unending blessings' (Ps. 21:6). One of the blessings that I've heard very few Christians talk about is what awaits us in the future. For the believer in Jesus –

WE HAVE THE BLESSING OF FUTURE REWARDS!

1. Bo Sanchez, 2013, 'Don't try to get all your rewards on earth.' Facebook, January 14, 2013. https://www.facebook.com/BrotherBoSanchez/photos/a.316550135235/10151390850135236/?type=3

Our culture is a 'What's in it for me?' environment. The follower of Jesus might overreact to the attitude of expecting payback and minimize or overlook the clear biblical teaching of future rewards for faithful service.

The Blessing

Lost people have no reason to expect any rewards from God at the judgment. And that is sad. For the believer, there ought to be a healthy expectation of the Lord's commendation when he or she stands before Him after this life.

The Bible

Two biblical texts leap out to me when thinking about one's good works and the possibility of future rewards. In Matthew 7:21-23, we read of those who *did good things* but *did not know the Lord*:

> Not everyone who says to me, 'Lord, Lord,' will enter the kingdom of heaven, but only the one who does the will of my Father who is in heaven. Many will say to me on that day, 'Lord, Lord, did we not prophesy in your name and in your name drive out demons and in your name perform many miracles?' Then I will tell them plainly, 'I never knew you. Away from me, you evildoers!'

Entering the kingdom of heaven is based on a relationship with Christ – not on one's good works.

However, in the parable of the sheep and goats in Matthew 25, we learn the following:

1. All of humanity ('all the nations', v. 32) is divided into two and only two groups: the sheep and the goats.

2. The sheep are commended by the Father for caring for the needs of others, even though the sheep weren't aware that the good works they were doing were being done unto Christ (vv. 37-39).

3. The sheep are called 'blessed by my Father' and are given the inheritance of the kingdom which has been prepared for them since the creation of the world (v. 34).

4. The goats are told by the King to depart from him, are cursed, and are banished into the eternal fire prepared for the devil and his angels (v. 41). Why? Because they did not do any of those good works (v. 45).

5. The parable is summarized with the somber words: 'Then they [the goats] will go away to eternal punishment; but the righteous [the sheep] to eternal life' (v. 46).

So the Bible teaches that we don't earn salvation by our good works. But our good works (after conversion) show our relationship with Christ.

ACTION STEPS

1. There are many other texts that talk about the believer receiving rewards for faithfulness. Look up each day this week two of the following passages and take some notes: Colossians 3:23-24; Romans 2:6; 1 Corinthians 15:58; Galatians 6:9; Matthew 25:21; James 1:12; Matthew 6:1-2, 20; Hebrews 11:6; Revelation 22:12; 1 Timothy 6:17-19; 1 Corinthians 3:8-15; 2 Corinthians

5:10; Matthew 16:27; Jeremiah 17:10; Genesis 15:1; Proverbs 11:18; Matthew 5:11-12; Luke 6:38; 2 Timothy 4:8; Mark 9:41; 2 John 1:8; etc. [Psalm 17:14 speaks of the wicked as: 'those of this world whose reward is in this life.']

2. Read through the epistle of James and answer the following question: Do James and the Apostle Paul differ on how one is saved? What is James' point about good works?

3. Read a chapter or two of Randy Alcorn's excellent book *Heaven: Biblical Answers to Common Questions about Our Eternal Home.*

4. PRAYER So, how do I pray for my unsaved friend? I will pray for my friend to think about the final judgment and how he needs to be 'in Christ' to receive any rewards.

→ BLESSING 22 ←

The Blessing of a Fearless Intellectual Life

Whenever someone tries to deny the truth, ultimately, reality betrays him (Greg Koukl).[1]

My heart grieves for my friend Mike who thinks he's right with God, but isn't. And as I've been praying for him, I'm becoming more aware of what I have that he doesn't – yet. And the blessing list includes many more items than simply salvation, as fundamental as that is.

Another blessing that I have as a believer doesn't seem to get much publicity among the people of God. Perhaps we are afraid. Maybe we aren't sure of this blessing. But I believe we need to recognize and pursue this gift. I believe my saved friends –

WE HAVE THE BLESSING OF A FEARLESS INTELLECTUAL LIFE!

---

1. Gregory Koukl, *Tactics: A Game Plan for Discussing Your Christian Convictions* (Grand Rapids, MI: Zondervan, 2009), p. 144.

If biblical Christianity is really true, then *all* other worldviews are somehow flawed. Other religions and philosophies deny the reality of the biblical God, salvation alone through faith in Christ alone, man's need of redemption, the trustworthiness of the Bible, etc. We are not being arrogant when we take our stand on the absolute truth of the Christian worldview.

The Blessing

Some scholars have said that the early Christians 'out thought the world!' I'm not so sure that's true of our present generation – but it could be. The follower of Jesus should be able to talk to anyone about the gospel without fear. We should not be afraid to vigorously debate worldviews for we are not engaged in comparative mythology, but truth. And when we don't have an answer to a hard question, we go and do our homework!

However, I feel that many Christians think of their faith as so personal that all they can share is their peace and happiness in Jesus. And that's it. The late scholar Carl Henry once said, 'Your relationship to Christ must be personal. *But it dare not be private!*'[2]

The Christian worldview is based on facts and evidence. The believers in the first century were not afraid to debate the messiahship of Jesus in the Jewish synagogues or argue the gospel among the intellectual elite of the day (Acts 17).

---

2. Website: larrydixon.wordpress.com https://larrydixon.wordpress.com/2022/02/16/bless-ed-52-blessings-your-lost-friend-doesnt-have-and-what-you-can-do-about-it-part-22/. Accessed September 16, 2022. No further information available.

Followers of Jesus are in a cooperative ministry with God the Holy Spirit. Our job is to present the best case we can for Jesus Christ and biblical Christianity. The Holy Spirit's job is to bring conviction to the heart of the unsaved. We work together. We are to seek to *convince*; His job is to *convict*.

The Bible

Jesus did not hesitate to declare Himself as 'the way, the truth, and the life' (John 14:6). He even dogmatically claimed that 'no one comes to the Father except through me.' His claims stand up under the intense scrutiny of this unbelieving world – and the Christian has the privilege of carefully responding to those who don't believe. We read in 1 Peter 3:15-16:

> But in your hearts revere Christ as Lord. Always be prepared to give an answer to everyone who asks you to give the reason for the hope that you have. But do this with gentleness and respect, keeping a clear conscience, so that those who speak maliciously against your good behavior in Christ may be ashamed of their slander.

This is a powerful text to challenge the believer to get out of his Lazyboy and get in the battle. No fear. And he or she is to be ready to respond to questions that are provoked in their unbelieving friends by the conduct and gentleness of the believer.

ACTION STEPS

1. Be risky this week and ask your unbelieving friend the following question: 'If you could list only one intellectual reason for not believing the gospel, what

would it be?' Ask him or her to give you one week to prepare an answer to their question.

2. Commit yourself to read 1 Peter 3:13-16 every day this week. And take notes on what you learn each day.

3. Read *Tactics: A Game Plan for Discussing Your Christian Convictions* by Gregory Koukl. This would be one of my top ten books for helping believers share their faith. Consider reading this book with a friend and discussing it together.

4. PRAYER So, how do I pray for my unsaved friend? I speak the gospel unashamedly and get ready to take questions. I read what I need to read in secular literature and I keep myself soaking in God's Word and crying out to His Spirit to bring conviction to my friend. And I pray that he or she will open their heart to the truth.

→ BLESSING 23 ←

The Blessing of a Healthy Sense of Humor

'Please don't do that, Jim!' I said out loud in my car as I listened to my favorite stand-up comedian resort to four-letter words to entertain his audience. Considered by many to be a 'clean stand-up comedian', he gave into vulgarity and coarseness. And I found it sad.

I have a vested interest in stand-up comedy. My son and I took stand-up comedy lessons together a few years ago and I know how hard it is to write a good sketch. He and I (and maybe one other guy) were the only clean students in the class. Effective comedy needn't be abusive or demeaning or gross, especially for the one who believes that God gave us a sense of humor.

I have unsaved friends who have a great sense of humor, but others who have no boundaries. For that reason, I thank God for laughter and would suggest that one blessing all believers (potentially) have is –

WE POSSESS A HEALTHY SENSE OF HUMOR

The Blessing

While it is certainly true that Jesus was 'a man of sorrows,' we should not conclude that He was not also a man of great joy and laughter (see Elton Trueblood's excellent book *The Humor of Christ*). The blessing of believers is that we can laugh, for we have been created by a God of great humor.

The Bible

The Bible teaches that 'A cheerful heart is good medicine, but a crushed spirit dries up the bones' (Prov. 17:22). The psalmist says of the Lord's rescue, 'Our mouths were filled with laughter, our tongues with songs of joy' (Ps. 126:2). We're told that there is 'a time to weep and a time to laugh, a time to mourn and a time to dance …' (Eccles. 3:4). Job's friend Bildad erringly challenges Job to confess his 'sins', promising that the Lord 'will yet fill your mouth with laughter and your lips with shouts of joy' (Job 8:21).

The Bible condemns the laughter of the wicked. We read of laughter which often mocks, scoffs, or derides (Gen. 21:9; 38:23; 39:14, 17; 2 Chron. 30:10; Ps. 52:6; 80:6; Prov. 1:26; Ezek. 23:32; Hab. 1:10).

We even have a text which says of the Lord laughing 'at the wicked, for he knows their day is coming' (Ps. 37:13). There is also the laughter of not believing God's promise shown in the response of Abraham and Sarah (Gen. 17:17 and 18:12).

Lewis' *The Screwtape Letters* speaks about four types of humor. Some advance 'the Enemy's (Christ's) cause'; some advance the cause of the demons. The first type—

JOY—is the one most detested by the demons, for it makes others feel warm and wanted.

The second type is FUN which Screwtape describes as 'a sort of emotional froth arising from the play instinct.' FUN can divert humans from something else which Christ would like them to be feeling or doing. Fun is great, but it can also be distracting.

The third type of humor—THE JOKE PROPER—is usually why we laugh at things. Something takes us by surprise or 'turns on a sudden perception of incongruity.' But the joke can become a kind of armor that keeps us from admitting a fault or facing possible shame. This type of humor can be weaponized, allowing us to cover our malice.

The fourth type of humor is FLIPPANCY, a kind of humor which prevents serious dialogue and treats critical subjects (sexual purity before marriage, male leadership in the home, a biblical worldview) as a joke, mere punchlines. Hollywood and the internet thrive on flippancy and we become inoculated to it.[1]

ACTION STEPS

1. This week, watch a sit-com on TV and analyze the kind of humor that is presented there. Into which of Lewis' categories does that humor seem to fit? How would you criticize that kind of humor?

2. Take time this week to read through one of the gospels and ask, 'Where does the humor of the Lord Jesus

---

1. C. S. Lewis, *The Screwtape Letters* (Scribner Paper Fiction; Rev edition, 1982), chapter 11.

show up?' Compare your notes with another believer doing the same.

3. Read the article 'God Laughs Out Loud to Quiet Our Fears' by David Mathis.[2]

4. PRAYER So how do I pray for my lost friend? I pray that my sense of humor will be alive and real and reflective of the God who created us to laugh and experience life. And I pray for my friend to get serious with the Lord so he can also experience real joy.

---

2. https://www.desiringgod.org/articles/god-laughs-out-loud-to-quiet-our-fears

⇢ BLESSING 24 ⇠

The Blessing of a Balanced Perspective on Possessions

Someone asked a question of John Davison Rockefeller, Sr., an American business magnate and philanthropist whose net worth in the early 19th Century was $418 billion. The question was, 'How much money does a person really need?' And he reportedly answered, 'Just a little bit *more!*'[1]

My friend Mike, who has not yet trusted Christ as his Savior, is fairly wealthy and quite generous. He has plenty of earthly treasures, but, as of yet, isn't storing up treasures in heaven as Jesus teaches.

This reminds me that we believers –

WE POSSESS A BALANCED PERSPECTIVE ON POSSESSIONS!

I'm not saying that my friends are greedy or materialistic, but many of them lack a biblical perspective on what they

---

1. As told in Michael Batnik, 'Just a Little Bit More.' The Irrelevant Investor. March 4, 2019. https://theirrelevantinvestor.com/2019/03/04/just-a-little-bit-more/

own. This is also true of many of us Jesus followers. In a sense, our possessions often possess us.

The Blessing

God's Word is clear that He is not anti-matter, that what we own isn't really ours, that things are not to be more valued than people, and that He uses material blessings for His glory. We are stewards, not only of His grace, but of the gifts He gives to use for Him. Some preachers have said that Jesus taught more about money than He did about heaven. I've not checked that out, but He does warn of greed (Luke 12:15) and Scripture confronts us with the temptation of esteeming others based on their financial status (see James 2).

The Bible

The Bible provides very specific principles about our possessions. Let's think about Jesus' teaching in Matthew 6:19-21 –

> Do not store up for yourselves treasures on earth, where moths and vermin destroy, and where thieves break in and steal. But store up for yourselves treasures in heaven, where moths and vermin do not destroy, and where thieves do not break in and steal. For where your treasure is, there your heart will be also.

There are some very clear principles in this passage. We must be careful where we store our wealth (v. 19). Earthly wealth is susceptible to bugs and burglars. Treasures stored up in heaven aren't in danger of being destroyed or stolen. One's treasure and one's heart are intimately connected to one another.

Other truths in Scripture about our possessions include: (1) All that we have we have from the Lord (1 Cor. 4:7); (2) Even your own life has been bought at the price of Christ's blood (1 Cor. 6:19-20); (3) One's life and value are not dependent on what one owns (Luke 12:15); (4) We are to learn to be content in either poverty or material abundance (Phil. 4:11-12); (5) We should be ready to share practically with those in need (Eph. 4:28); (6) Earthly wealth can keep people out of the kingdom of God (Mark 10:17-31); and (7) God is not anti-possessions (Acts 4:32-37; 5:1-11).

ACTION STEPS

1. Take this week to carefully read over the story in Mark 10 of the rich young ruler. When Jesus commanded him to give all he had to the poor, he walked away. Why? How would one prove that Jesus was teaching him he could be saved by his good works?

2. Corrie Ten Boom is reported to have said, 'I have learned to hold things loosely so that it won't hurt so much when God takes it away.'[2] When you think of your material goods, fill in the following blank: 'It would hurt really badly if God were to take away my _____.' Then mentally put that something under the Lordship of Christ.

3. Read an article or two each day this week by Dave Ramsey[3] on financial health. Take a few notes and share with another believer.

---

2. I couldn't find the original source for this quote but it has been going around the internet attributed to her for a long time.

3. https://www.ramseysolutions.com/articles?author=dave-ramsey#feed-content

4. PRAYER. Unbelievers watch us so it is important to be generous with what God has given us. Pray that your friend will see that for you the Giver is much more important than the gifts. And pray for all your lost friends that they would seek the Lord 'who richly provides us with everything for our enjoyment' (1 Tim. 6:17).

→ BLESSING 25 ←

The Blessing of an Awareness of Spiritual Warfare

There are two equal and opposite errors into which our race can fall about the devils. One is to disbelieve in their existence. The other is to believe, and to feel an excessive and unhealthy interest in them (C. S. Lewis).[1]

Awareness. That's what I need more of as a believer. And I'm receiving more awareness of my many blessings 'in Christ' as I think about my lost friend Mike.

One of the blessings I have doesn't appear on the surface to be a positive one like a permanent joy or a place in God's family. But it is a blessing nonetheless, because it's true and essential for the follower of Jesus. And my lost friends don't have it. From my perspective we believers –

WE HAVE AN AWARENESS OF SPIRITUAL WARFARE!

---

1. C. S. Lewis, *Screwtape Letters* (New York: HarperCollins, 2009), ix.

The Blessing

'Wait a minute!,' some might say. 'Are you talking about demons and the devil and stuff?!' Yes. The Bible is quite clear that the Christian has a diabolical army opposing him, tempting him, blinding him to the spiritual battle he is in.

The Bible

We are not suggesting that the believer needs to cower in fear, thinking that there's a demon behind every bush. But there is much more going on in life than we can presently see. The Apostle Paul says in Ephesians 6:12, 'For our struggle is not against flesh and blood, but against the rulers, against the authorities, against the powers of this dark world and against the spiritual forces of evil in the heavenly realms.' Notice from this passage that we are in a struggle, a battle. And our enemy is not other human beings. Our enemy is described as 'the authorities,' 'the powers of this dark world,' and 'the spiritual forces of evil.' This is no time for a kind of spiritual pacifism. We are at war!

Here is some of what the Scriptures teach about spiritual warfare: (1) The devil is a real spirit being who has an army at his disposal to oppose God and the things of God (Gen. 3; Rev. 12); (2) His purpose is to tempt mankind into disobeying God and to entrap the believer (he is on the prowl looking for someone to devour, 1 Pet. 5:8); (3) Believers are to be aware of the devil's tricks and to oppose him (we are to be cognizant of the devil's ways of operating, 2 Cor. 2:11); (4) The devil is a defeated foe and will one day be cast into the

lake of fire forever (a place prepared for him, Matt. 25;
Rev. 20); (5) Christians are to focus upon the Lord and
resist the devil and he will flee from them (James 4:7).

Much more could be said about spiritual warfare. But
the believer is not at peace in this world. And he needs
to get in the battle, calling upon the Lord for strength
and courage in face of his enemies: the world, the flesh,
and the devil.

ACTION STEPS

1. Read over each day this week the devil's original
   temptation of Adam and Eve in Genesis 3. What is
   his *modus operandi* (his way of working)? It appears
   he has not deviated from the way he seeks to bring
   believers down. Have you sensed any of his techniques
   being used on you? How do you respond biblically to
   his tempting you?

2. C. S. Lewis says we make two errors about the devil:
   we either think about him too little or we think about
   him too much. How do you find a biblical balance?
   Discuss this question with another believer this week.

3. Much has been written about spiritual warfare – and
   not all of it biblical. A balanced perspective is set
   forth in the short book *Territorial Spirits and World
   Evangelisation: A Biblical, Historical and Missio-
   logical Critique of Strategic-Level Spiritual Warfare*
   by Chuck Lowe.

4. PRAYER So, how do I pray for my unsaved friend? I
   somehow let it be known that I am in a war and must

resist a supernatural enemy. And I pray for my friend who needs to move from being a child of the devil (John 8:44; Eph. 2:12; Acts 13:10) to being a child of God (John 1:12)!

The Blessing of a Biblical Understanding of Good Works

John Wesley, the circuit-riding preacher, once said, 'Do all the good you can, in all the ways you can, to all the souls you can, in every place you can, at all the times you can, with all the zeal you can, as long as ever you can.'[1]

'One good deed a day!' was the Boy Scout motto that I tried to follow as a youth. My unsaved friends often try to do good, to be kind, to help when possible. But I have learned as a believer *why* we should do good works.

One of our clearest blessings as believers is –

WE HAVE A BIBLICAL UNDERSTANDING OF GOOD WORKS!

When our house burned down in 2003, my unsaved tennis buddies *literally* gave me the shirts off their

---

1. This quotation is commonly attributed to John Wesley, but its first appearance was a footnote in George Eayrs (ed.), *Letters of John Wesley* (Hodder and Stoughton, 1915), p. 423. The footnote refers to it as 'Wesley's rule' but there is nothing in Wesley's own writings to this effect.

backs! They provided meals, words of encouragement, and practical help for which we were most grateful. So what's the blessing I have which my lost friends don't have?

The Blessing

What they don't have is the *why* of doing good works. For those outside Christ, many live good, moral lives trying to earn credit with God. They envision a large scale in front of God's throne weighing their good works versus their bad works. And they hope beyond hope that the good works' side will win the day.

But no one can do enough good works to merit God's forgiveness. Trying to earn God's grace is an insult to the amazing sacrifice which the Son of God made when He gave His life on the cross for our sins.

The Bible

Believers in Jesus know they are to do good works, not to earn or even keep their salvation, but to honor God and to serve the world. We read in Ephesians 2:8-10:

> For it is by grace you have been saved, through faith—and this is not from yourselves, it is the gift of God—not by works, so that no one can boast. For we are God's handiwork, created in Christ Jesus to do good works, which God prepared in advance for us to do.

Salvation is not a matter of human works, but of receiving God's grace by faith. However, after salvation, there are good works which God has prepared in advance for us to do! For the believer, the question is, are you doing them? For the unbeliever, you first need to get into God's family through the work of Christ. Then you can work on Ephesians 2:10!

Many passages speak about the believer's doing good works, such as James 4:17 ('If anyone, then, knows the good they ought to do and doesn't do it, it is sin for them.'); Romans 12:21 ('Do not be overcome by evil, but overcome evil with good.'); Galatians 6:10 ('Therefore, as we have opportunity, let us do good to all people, especially to those who belong to the family of believers.'); and Titus 2:14 ('... who gave himself for us to redeem us from all wickedness and to purify for himself a people that are his very own, eager to do what is good.').

Unsaved people do good works because they are made in the image of God, they care about the needs of others, and they seek to live 'good' lives. And we may commend them for the good they do. But that's not salvation.

ACTION STEPS

1. Has your Christianity become primarily verbal (words, not works)? This week, go over Ephesians 2:8-10 with another believer, asking what actions you as a Jesus follower ought to take in light of that passage of Scripture.

2. Every day this week, look for one good deed to do for the Lord. It might be allowing another car into traffic instead of insisting they wait for you. It might involve helping a neighbor with their yard work. It might be buying lunch for a panhandler that you

would normally look past. Ask the Lord to guide you into each day's good deed.

3. Read the article 'Good Works and the Christian Life' by John Tweeddale.[2] Take some notes on the article and discuss it with another Christian friend.

4. PRAYER So, how do I pray for my lost friend Mike? I pray first for myself that my faith would not just be verbal, that I would show my relationship to Christ by what I *do* for others. For Mike, I would pray that he would abandon the idea of earning God's favor by his own works and would cast himself on Christ whose work was perfect.

---

2. https://www.ligonier.org/learn/articles/good-works-christian-life

→ BLESSING 27 ←

The Blessing of a Godly Routine

You will never change your life until you change something you do daily. The secret of your success is found in your daily routine (John C. Maxwell).[1]

I love being retired! I recommend retirement to all my friends. Being retired gives me sufficient time to pursue what I believe to be a *godly* routine. And pursuing that routine is a blessing.

The Blessing

Life is not meant to be lived 100 per cent spontaneously. We need routine. We need habits which we pursue. We need discipline to make good choices with our time and energy. We Jesus followers are blessed in that –

WE HAVE A GODLY ROUTINE!

Here's my morning routine: I wake up about 5:30 a.m. (I'm in bed by 9:30 p.m. the night before), make coffee, and settle into my LazyBoy. I check my email, look at

---

1. Found at https://www.johnmaxwell.com/blog/it-all-comes-down-to-what-you-do-daily/January 14, 2015. Accessed January 26, 2023.

our Amazon account (we sell about ten used books a day), and then make my chess moves on chess.com (I lose internationally). I then dive into my devotional reading.

My friend Frank and I have been reading Scripture together each week for the last couple of years. Our practice has been explained in my blog (larrydixon. wordpress.com). Another group of brothers read a different chapter of Scripture every day, so I have to read that second assignment. I write out my prayer for the day and am then finished with my daily devotional reading. Then I work on sermons or my blog or emails.

My wife Linda wakes up about 6:30 a.m. and, when she comes into our sun room, I kiss her good morning and ask the same question every day, 'Would you like a cup of coffee?' And she always says 'Yes, as a matter of fact, I would!' I then take my shower, weigh myself (she says she wants to see less of me), and then report my weight to my wife. My morning ritual is done when she and I sit on the couch and pray together.

As far as I know, my friend Mike doesn't read God's Word, doesn't write out his prayer for the day, doesn't pray with his wife. He probably just has his breakfast, maybe cycles a few miles on his Peloton, greets his family, and goes to work. That's not bad, but he's missing the kind of godly routine that allows God the Holy Spirit to change his life, reorder his priorities and make him more like Jesus.

The Blessing

We're really talking about what are called the spiritual disciplines. These include meditation, solitude, worship, prayer, Bible reading, etc.

The Bible

The early Christians 'devoted themselves to the apostles' teaching and to fellowship, to the breaking of bread and to prayer' (Acts 2:42). Some of their disciplines were practiced in the community of believers. Individually, we see a person like Daniel, whose daily ritual of prayer (three times a day) put his life in jeopardy (Dan. 6:10). Daily rituals are encouraged by such texts as Matthew 6:11 (asking for our daily bread), Luke 9:23 (we're to take up our cross daily and follow Him), and Hebrews 3:13 (we're to encourage each other daily lest sin harden us). In fact, our regular practices may affect our witness. Paul says in 1 Thessalonians 4:12 'that your daily life may win the respect of outsiders and so that you will not be dependent on anybody.'

ACTION STEPS

1. Read the article 'What Are the Spiritual Disciplines?', an interview with Don Whitney who wrote the book *Spiritual Disciplines for the Christian Life.*[2] Pick one of the disciplines to practice each day this week.

2. If you struggle to have a daily quiet time (time spent reading God's Word and praying), write out a serious prayer of commitment which you will pray each day this week for God's help.

3. Read Richard J. Foster's book *Celebration of Discipline: The Path to Spiritual Growth.* You need not agree with

---

2. https://www.desiringgod.org/interviews/what-are-spiritual-disciplines

everything Foster says, but you will benefit greatly from his work.

4. PRAYER My friend Mike has no reason to pursue the spiritual disciplines or a godly routine, for he is not yet in the family of God. But, maybe, one day he will be! How do I pray for my unsaved friend? First, I pray for myself that I would settle into a godly routine that exalts God's Word and opens my heart and life to God the Holy Spirit for needed change. Then, I pray for my friend to come to Christ and, perhaps, for opportunities to share with him what I've learned from God's Word that morning!

✧ BLESSING 28 ✧

The Blessing of a Searching to Find the God Who Hides Himself

Everything is made to center upon the initial act of 'accepting' Christ (a term, incidentally, which is not found in the Bible) and we are not expected thereafter to crave any further revelation of God to our souls. We have been snared in the coils of a spurious logic which insists that if we have found Him we need no more seek Him (A. W. Tozer).[1]

After working a night job at UPS during my graduate studies, I would come home early in the morning, kiss my wife and young children hello, and then, when our son and daughter were out of the room, I'd hide in the linen closet. The kids would come into the kitchen, notice my absence, and ask Mom, 'Where's Dad?' Mom would lie. All moms lie. And she would say, 'I have no idea!' Then the kids knew they would have to find me. They knew immediately that Dad had initiated a game of hide and seek.

---

1. A. W. Tozer, *The Pursuit of God: A 31-Day Experience* (Chicago: Moody, 2021), p. 38.

After they had searched the house for me (I could see their little sneakers through the slats in the linen closet), I would then come out of the, uh, closet and sit drinking coffee with my wife. They would ask where I had been hiding. I finally told them about the linen closet hiding place when they each turned eighteen.

On one occasion, I came home from my night job, kissed my wife and children good morning, and hid when their backs were turned. I could hear them running around the house trying to find me. And then there was silence. I came out of my hiding place and went to find them. They were in the basement watching cartoons.

They were quite happy no longer seeking Dad. I was devastated.

One of the many blessings for the believer is that we are never finished with our quest to know the Lord. And we should commit ourselves to the blessing that –

WE SEARCH FOR THE GOD WHO HIDES HIMSELF!

The Blessing
One of the many blessings in being a believer in Jesus is the fact that we can search for the God 'who hides himself' (Isa. 45:15). He doesn't play games with us, but longs for us to long for Him. We hurt ourselves and grieve God when our attitude is 'I've got salvation. I've got God. Now I can move on.'

The Bible
As the God who sometimes hides Himself, the Lord waits for us to pursue Him. Job spoke of the Lord in

the following words: 'But if he remains silent, who can condemn him? If he hides his face, who can see him? Yet he is over individual and nation alike ...' (Job 34:29). In beautiful King James language, the psalmist writes, 'Why standest thou afar off, O Lᴏʀᴅ? why hidest thou thyself in times of trouble?' (Ps. 10:1 ᴋᴊᴠ). In the midst of catastrophe, the psalmist does not hesitate to express his question, 'Wherefore hidest thou thy face, and forgettest our affliction and our oppression?' (Ps. 44:24 ᴋᴊᴠ). 'Why do you ... hide your face from me?', he asks in Psalm 88:14.

The bottom line is that God wants us to seek Him, to thirst for Him, to long to know Him deeper and deeper. The nature of an intimate relationship is that it is ever-growing, maturing, developing. Tozer is right that many of us have given up on our quest to know God simply because we have gotten salvation.

ACTION STEPS

1. This week, analyze Tozer's statement with another believer. You might need to look up the term 'spurious' (I had to). Although I disagree with his implication that the idea of 'accepting Christ' isn't biblical, there is so much in his statement that merits serious reflection. What might be a more biblical expression than 'accepting Christ'?

2. What are some biblical reasons that God sometimes hides Himself? Were Job's friends right that God was hiding Himself from Job because of Job's sins? For what reasons might the Lord hide Himself from you?

3. Read A. W. Tozer's classic *The Pursuit of God* with a close friend and discuss each of the chapters together.

4. PRAYER So, how do I pray for my unsaved friend? I try to make it clear that, although I now belong to the Lord through Christ, I've just begun to seek Him, to know Him deeply. And I pray that kind of longing will get a hold of my lost friend.

✦ BLESSING 29 ✦

The Blessing of a Passion for Souls

'When I was twelve,' writes Sylvester Madison, 'my best friend and I broke a window playing baseball. We looked around to see if anyone had seen us. No one was in sight except my younger brother. We went over and offered him a piece of candy not to tell. He refused it. "I'll give you my baseball," I said. "No." "Then what about *my* baseball and my new glove?" my friend added. "No!" "Well, what *do* you want?" "I wanna tell"' (*Readers' Digest*).

As I think about my unsaved friend Mike, God is reminding me of the many blessings I enjoy – or should enjoy – that he does not yet have. One blessing that occurs to me might sound strange, but I believe is a marker of a serious follower of Jesus. I believe my saved friends and I –

WE HAVE A PASSION FOR SOULS!

The Blessing

What do we mean by 'a passion for souls'? We mean that the follower of Jesus is greatly concerned with the spiritual welfare of *everyone* he or she meets or knows.

127

If the Bible is true that every human being is headed either to hell or to heaven, then the right passion, the crystal clear passion of the Christian, must be the gospel. Proverbs 11:30 puts it well – 'The fruit of the righteous is a tree of life; and he that winneth souls is wise' (KJV).

I'm certainly not criticizing my lost friends for the passion that they have for their families. I'm grateful when my friend Mike expresses his desire to be a good husband and father. But what ought to be the highest priority in a human being's life is knowing God and longing for others to know Him.

Jesus says in John 17, 'Now this is eternal life: that they know you, the only true God, and Jesus Christ, whom you have sent' (v. 3). Eternal life is not simply unending existence, but a quality of life in knowing and following the God of the universe.

The Bible

A passion for souls involves the following elements: (1) A clear recognition that man without Christ is lost (John 8:22-24); (2) A daily discipline of praying for those who are outside of Christ ('As for me, far be it from me that I should sin against the Lord by failing to pray for you.' 1 Sam. 12:23); (3) Eyes open to opportunities to share a bit of the gospel on every occasion ('Preach the word; be prepared in season and out of season; correct, rebuke and encourage – with great patience and careful instruction.' 2 Tim. 4:2); (4) An awareness of being a stench to some and an aroma to others ('For we are to God the pleasing aroma of Christ among those who are being saved and those who are perishing. To the one we are an aroma that brings death; to the other, an aroma that brings life. And who is equal to such a task?' 2 Cor. 2:15-16); (5) A commitment to doing the homework necessary to answer any questions which are keeping a person from believing the gospel (see Acts 17, where the Apostle Paul knows pagan literature so he could speak to the philosophers of his day).

ACTION STEPS

1. Begin a prayer 'hit list' this week, naming those whom you long to come to know Christ.

2. Spend time this week with a believer who is passionate about sharing the gospel. Take out someone who has the gift of evangelism—or at least a heart for the lost—for lunch and interview them. How did they come to know Christ? What do they find most helpful in sharing the gospel with others?

3. Read my short book *Unlike Jesus: Let's Stop Unfriending the World*. List several ways that we can be like the Lord Jesus in being a 'friend of sinners.'

4. PRAYER So, how do I pray for my lost friends? I pray for myself that I would not settle for a watered-down, minimal concern for the eternal welfare of others. I want my evangelistic zeal to be white-hot, but wise in its expression. And I pray for each friend that he would see that eternity is a long time to be wrong about Jesus. And that he would trust Him as his Savior and get passionate about others doing the same.

The Blessing of a Balanced View of Technology

It has become appallingly obvious that our technology has exceeded our humanity (Albert Einstein).[1]

I've been blessed to travel to developing countries to teach theology to national church leaders. My travels have a way of making me extremely thankful for the wealth and comfort most of us enjoy in the West. One aspect of our wealth—technology—is enjoyed by many. Although it has brought many blessings to our culture, technology is fraught with many dangers. Distraction is a very obvious example. I will no longer walk or ride my bike *with* traffic because I'm afraid of distracted drivers busy checking their phones who might simply run over me.

My lost friend Mike enjoys many of the same gadgets and gizmos our technological society has bestowed upon

---

1. Charles Harper, Jr., *Spiritual Formation: 100 Perspectives on Science and Religion* (Philadelphia: Templeton Foundation Press, 2006), p. 515.

us. But for those of us who follow Christ, it ought to be said of us –

WE HAVE A BALANCED VIEW OF TECHNOLOGY!

I'm not suggesting that my friend Mike is addicted to video games or anything of the sort. Although one wonders if this is mostly true of our entire culture. But I don't believe he's aware of the dark side of new innovations. As someone has cynically written, 'Modern technology has not made man better morally but only more powerful in his wickedness.'

The bottom line is that all of life should be used for the glory of God. And, sadly, much of technology has one and only one purpose: entertainment. 'Amusement'—a term which literally means 'no thinking'—seems to be one of the highest goals of our culture. And, indeed, hardly a thought is given to bingeing for hours watching a TV series or spending inordinate amounts of money to install the latest video equipment.

The Blessing

The fact is that we are responsible for how we use technology. We are challenged in 1 Corinthians 10 to live our lives carefully before God: 'Whether therefore ye eat, or drink, or whatsoever ye do, do all to the glory of God' (v. 31, KJV).

We can—and should—use our technology for blessing others and for advancing God's kingdom. Entertainment is not evil in itself. But it must not be all-consuming. One cynic wrote about Western culture: 'When historians of a future generation look back on American culture, they will sneer and say, "They entertained themselves to death.'"

The Bible

What does God's Word have to say about the believer and technology? The Apostle Paul, writing in a culture without electricity, cell phones, television, or the internet, made it quite clear that 'whatever you do, whether in word or deed, do it all in the name of the Lord Jesus, giving thanks to God the Father through him' (Col. 3:17). His 'whatever', inspired by the Holy Spirit, applies to every aspect of life. This certainly includes social media, which is sometimes anything but social! Paul's overarching passion in life—'that I may know him, and the power of his resurrection, and the fellowship of his sufferings, being made conformable unto his death' – found in Philippians 3 verse 10 (KJV) shouldn't be Paul's passion alone. Every believer in Christ should have the same goal.

ACTION STEPS

1. Does the idea of unplugging for twenty-four hours terrify you? Take one day this week and either completely cut out or severely limit your screen time. What conclusions did such an experiment bring to your mind? Would you share some of those with a friend this week?

2. Investigate how you can use technology to encourage those who are in ministry. Perhaps a well-timed text or email. Perhaps a brief Zoom call to a missionary

friend. You might find just the right short video online to help a struggling friend with a problem.

3. Read the short online article 'Technology Can be Blessing, Curse to Students' written by Alexandra Pittman in 2012 and apply some of his concerns to the Christian life this week.[2]

4. PRAYER So, how do I pray for my unsaved friend? I make conscious choices not to allow technology to have power over me. I will take advantage of any technology which advances our friendship. And I pray for my friend to understand that salvation finds its source in Jesus, not in technological advancements.

---

2. https://www.ucf.edu/news/technology-can-be-blessing-curse-to-students/

❧ BLESSING 31 ❦

The Blessing of a Vigilance about Temptation

Only those who try to resist temptation know how strong it is ... We never find out the strength of the evil impulse inside us until we try to fight it: and Christ, because He was the only man who never yielded to temptation, is also the only man who knows to the full what temptation means – the only complete realist (C. S. Lewis).[1]

What are some temptations that you face as a believer? One of the blessings that I have as a follower of Christ is a sensitivity to the Lord. I don't want to embarrass my Savior, grieve the Holy Spirit, or hurt myself or my family by giving in to sin.

However, temptation is not sin. The Lord Jesus faced temptation, but turned away from the enticements of the Evil One. And believers face temptations all the time. But there is a blessing in being in the family of God and it is that –

---

1. C. S. Lewis, *Mere Christianity* (San Francisco: HarperOne, 2015), Section 11. 'Faith,' p. 77.

WE HAVE A VIGILANCE ABOUT TEMPTATION!

'Oh, no! Not another missionary!' I just learned that a long-term missionary had been caught cheating on his wife. They are now separated, getting intense counseling, but it seems unlikely that the marriage will survive. Christians aren't immune to temptation and sin.

The Blessing

So, one could argue that this blessing is a potential one (like many of the others). If we believers don't take advantage of this provision, we will fall, we will fail, and we will succumb to the enticements of the Evil One and our own wayward hearts. Vigilance about temptation is not automatic in the believer, but available through God's Word and God's Spirit.

The Bible

God's Word does not leave the believer in the dark when it comes to sin and its precursor – temptation. We read in Hebrews 4:15-16:

> For we do not have a high priest who is unable to empathize with our weaknesses, but we have one who has been tempted in every way, just as we are – yet he did not sin. Let us then approach God's throne of grace with confidence, so that we may receive mercy and find grace to help us in our time of need.

Please notice several key points brought out in this passage:

(1) Although the writer to the Hebrews uses negatives to make his point, the positive way to state verse 15

is: We have a high priest who is able to sympathize with our weaknesses! You and I, as children of God, will never be in a situation in which we can say, 'Jesus can't understand what I'm going through!'

(2) Jesus has been tempted in every way we are – yet He did not sin.

(3) We can approach God's throne of grace and find mercy and grace in our time of need. Our confidence is in His character and His desire to help us in our situation.

My lost friend Mike doesn't enjoy this kind of God-given vigilance. God may indeed show him mercy when he gives in to temptation, but he (as of yet) has no relationship to the Savior and should not expect to find help in his time of need. His greatest need is to repent of his sins and trust Christ for his salvation. Then Hebrews 4:15-16 will prove to be a great help to him!

ACTION STEPS

1. Take the time each day this week to pray through Hebrews 4:15-16. You might consider using a different translation each day. Write out several conclusions (at the end of the week) that you've come to about temptation.

2. Here's a tough assignment: Confess a temptation you are facing or a sin you've committed to another believer. James 5:16 commands the believer, 'Therefore confess your sins to each other and pray for each other

so that you may be healed. The prayer of a righteous person is powerful and effective.' Ask another Jesus follower to pray for you.

3. This is not meant to be self-serving, but your author has written an extensive treatment of temptation in his book *When Temptation Strikes: Gaining Victory Over Sin*.[2] You might consider reading a chapter or two in that book – and discussing it with a friend.

4. PRAYER So, how do I pray for my unsaved friends? I make it clear that I'm not above or beyond temptation and sin. I might share some of my struggles with my lost friends – and how Jesus as my High Priest helps me overcome temptation. And I pray for each friend that they would take temptation and sin seriously and bow their knee to the Savior.

---

2. Larry Dixon, *When Temptation Strikes: Gaining Victory Over Sin* (Fort Washington, PA: CLC Publications, 2011).

✦ BLESSING 32 ✦

The Blessing of Clarity about S-I-N

What a brutish master sin is, taking the joy from one's life, stealing money and health, giving promise of tomorrow's pleasures, and finally leading one onto the rotten planking that overlies the mouth of the pit (Jim Elliot).[1]

As we think about the many blessings we have as Christians, we fool ourselves if we believe we are beyond sin. We are still in a battle against temptation and sin and will be until we see Jesus.

The above quote, by the way, is from the missionary-martyr Jim Elliot. He's most famous for the challenging statement: 'He is no fool who gives what he cannot keep to gain what he cannot lose.'[2] From the introductory quote we can tell that Elliot was quite aware of sin's destructiveness, wasn't he?

---

1. Elisabeth Elliot, *The Shadow of the Almighty* (New York: Harper & Brothers; 7th edition, 1958), pp. 53-54.

2. Elisabeth Elliot, *Through Gates of Splendor* (Carol Stream, IL: Tyndale Momentum; 50th ed. edition, 1981), p. 172.

But what qualifies as 'sin'? Our culture muddies the waters of definition and is guilty of calling 'good' sin and 'sin' good. God's Word must be our dictionary for we believers –

WE HAVE A CLARITY ABOUT SIN!

The Blessing

Followers of Jesus have an authoritative source for identifying sin and turning from it. Granted, Christians have historically added to God's Word, describing some practices as sin (one thinks of dancing, for example) which aren't. We have also subtracted from God's Word, in excusing other practices (such as slavery) as not being sin. God's definitive Word is a blessing in that it gives us the truth about sin. We may not always act on this knowledge, but there it is – for our good. As a friend says, sin will hurt you and will hurt you bad.

The Bible

Scripture has so much to say about sin, from the Garden of Eden in Genesis 2–3 to the completion of human history in the book of Revelation, we learn of sin's destructive power. The Bible gives us specifics about sin that we must know and follow: (1) It is the Lord who defines sin (for example, the Ten Commandments, Exodus 20); (2) Sin is not just external acts, but includes internal thoughts and attitudes (Heb. 4:12); (3) All sin is deadly, so, although the Bible doesn't have a list of 'the seven deadly sins,' there are some lists of sins in God's Word (Prov. 6 is one example which is fascinating); (4) Sin is not just what one does, but what one doesn't do

(James 4:17); (5) Sin's remedy involves both confession (agreeing with God about our sin) and repentance (turning from sin) (1 John 1:9-10). Repentance may be described as siding with God the Holy Spirit who convicts us of our sin, rather than defending ourselves; (6) God's community, the church, is where sin is to be confronted and overcome (James 5:16); (7) We believers have the authority to declare sins forgiven or unforgiven based on a person's response to or rejection of the gospel (Matt. 16:19); etc.

We may use other words in talking about sin, but we should never excuse sin with our euphemisms ('My mistake!' or 'My bad!' or 'I just messed up! Can we move on?'). Sometimes the older words ('sin,' 'transgression,' 'iniquity') can be quite useful if they are clearly defined.

ACTION STEPS

1. Purpose this week before the Lord to allow His Word to be your dictionary when it comes to sin. Do a word study of a particular sin with which you struggle (pride, lust, laziness) and share your notes with another believer.

2. Let another follower of Jesus know that you will pray for them in their struggles and will gladly 'hear their confession.' We are priests to God, are we not? Communicate the truth that you will listen and will not condemn, but will share the truths of God's Word for the one who is struggling.

3. Please forgive one more reference to my book on temptation and sin (*When Temptation Strikes: Gaining*

Victory Over Sin). There is a great deal there about dealing with sin that you may find helpful.

4. PRAYER How do I pray for my lost friend? I pray that he may understand his own dire need of forgiveness from a holy God for his sins and may turn in repentance to Christ.

The Blessing of a Heartfelt, God-Directed Thankfulness

O Lord that lends me life, lend me a heart replete with thankfulness (William Shakespeare).[1]

I'm grateful for my friend Mike. Yes, he's as lost as lost can be. And I'm praying earnestly for him to come to know Christ. But thinking about him has got me thinking about … me. Well, not about me so much as about the many blessings I enjoy as a believer which my friend Mike does not yet enjoy.

Another blessing of which I'm becoming more aware is that of a heart full of gratitude toward God for all He has done for me. The normal Christian life should be characterized by the fact that we believers –

WE HAVE A HEARTFELT, GOD-DIRECTED THANKFULNESS!

I'm not saying my unsaved friends aren't thankful people. But how much of their thanksgiving is directed toward

---

1. *The Dramatic Works of William Shakespeare* (Phillips, Sampson and Company, 1851), William Shakespeare, Henry VI, Part One, Act One, Scene One, lines 21-22, p. 491.

the Lord? Apart from giving thanks at dinner, do they praise Him for life, for His mercy, for the gift of salvation? Not yet, as far as I can tell.

The Blessing

We live in an unthankful, entitled culture that demands its rights and expects only good things in life. But the believer is told: 'Give thanks in all circumstances; for this is God's will for you in Christ Jesus' (1 Thess. 5:18). The believer's default setting should be that of gratitude – for life, forgiveness, purpose, joy, and, yes, even trials.

The Bible

A lack of thankfulness is one characteristic of the lost person, according to Romans 1. In Paul's diatribe against fallen man, he writes, 'For although they knew God, they neither glorified him as God nor gave thanks to him, but their thinking became futile and their foolish hearts were darkened' (v. 21) Man's natural knowledge of God does not result either in his seeking to bring glory to God or in giving thanks to Him. And, as a result, man's thinking becomes futile and his heart is darkened. Futile thinking and a darkened heart are the result of choosing not to glorify God.

We read in 2 Timothy 3:2 that 'People will be lovers of themselves, lovers of money, boastful, proud, abusive, disobedient to their parents, ungrateful, unholy ...' A billboard in our area advertises in large letters, 'LOVE YOURSELF FIRST!' Notice that ingratitude is listed with other serious sins, including self-love, greed, boastfulness, and a lack of holiness.

Jesus advises His followers: 'But love your enemies, do good to them, and lend to them without expecting to get anything back. Then your reward will be great, and you will be children of the Most High, because he is kind to the ungrateful and wicked' (Luke 6:35). All human beings come into the world in ungrateful rebellion against the Lord. Thank God that He is kind to the ungrateful and wicked!

Believers in Jesus are to give thanks always for all things (Eph. 5:20). We are commanded to be thankful (Col. 3:15). When Christians seem confused about 'the will of God,' they need to be reminded of 1 Thessalonians 5:18 that says it is God's will for us to give thanks.

Giving thanks is equated with giving glory to God, as we see in the story of the ten lepers healed by Jesus (with only one returning to thank Him for the miracle) (Luke 17:16-19). At times it might seem difficult to do, but we are to offer 'supplications, prayers, intercessions, and giving of thanks ... for all men' (1 Tim. 2:1 KJV).

ACTION STEPS

1. We are never told to give thanks for evil, but we are to give thanks to the Lord who sovereignly controls nations and the affairs of men. Thank the Lord each day this week for a local or federal government leader. Pray for their spiritual life.

2. Think of and thank another believer who has encouraged you in the Lord. Email or text them if you can't meet with them face to face.

3. Write out a prayer of thankfulness to the Lord. List at least ten items for which you are thankful.

4. PRAYER So, how do I pray for my unsaved friend? I demonstrate by my life that I am grateful for all God's blessings to me. And I strategically pray for my lost friend that he would recognize his thankless natural state and turn to the Lord in gratitude for salvation.

⤜ BLESSING 34 ⤛

The Blessing of the Gift of True Freedom

Is freedom anything else than the right to live as we wish? Nothing else (Epictetus).[1]

The believer in Jesus has many blessings! And one of the reasons to have unsaved friends (in addition to our Savior being a friend of sinners) is that we are able to count the many gifts and advantages that we have in Christ which our lost friends don't yet have. We are those that the book of Revelation refers to as ones who have been 'freed ... from our sins by his blood' (Rev. 1:5).

So when it comes to followers of Jesus, I believe –

WE HAVE THE GIFT OF TRUE FREEDOM!

The Blessing

Freedom in Scripture is not the right to do what I want, but the power to do what I should. As someone has said,

---

1. Epictetus, *Sayings of Epictetus* (Boston, N. H. Dole, 1904), p. 101.

'Man's first duty is not to find freedom, but a Master!' Trusting Christ as one's Savior brings an incredible freedom which the world can only counterfeit. As the One who said, 'Then you will know the truth, and the truth will make you free' (John 8:32), He promised, 'if the Son sets you free, you will be free indeed' (John 8:36).

The Bible

Much of the epistle to the Galatians emphasizes the freedom the believer has in Christ. We read in Galatians 5 verse 1, 'It is for freedom that Christ has set us free. Stand firm, then, and do not let yourselves be burdened again by a yoke of slavery.'

The Messiah was prophesied as one who would provide freedom for those who believed in Him. We read of this prophecy in Isaiah 42 and hear Jesus apply those words to Himself in Luke 4 verse 18: 'The Spirit of the Lord is on me, because he has anointed me to proclaim good news to the poor. He has sent me to proclaim freedom for the prisoners and recovery of sight for the blind, to set the oppressed free ...'

The psalmist understood freedom and proclaimed: 'I will walk about in freedom, for I have sought out your precepts' (Ps. 119:45). Obedience to the precepts of God does not bring slavery, but a joy in freedom to live as we ought.

Even creation itself longs for the freedom that is promised; as we read in Romans 8:21: 'the creation itself will be liberated from its bondage to decay and brought into the freedom and glory of the children of God.'

The believer can come to God, as Ephesians says, 'with freedom and confidence' (3:12). Paul makes it clear as he thinks about his freedom in Christ—'"I have the right to do anything," you say—but not everything is beneficial.' (1 Cor. 10:23). Psalm 18 says, 'He brought me out into a spacious place; he rescued me because he delighted in me. ... You provide a broad path for my feet, so that my ankles do not give way' (vv. 19 and 36). There are no spiritually sprained ankles for those who, in freedom, walk in the spacious place and the broad path God provides.

ACTION STEPS

1. Imagine that you meet the Greek Stoic philosoher Epictetus one day on a bus (he's been dead since 135 B.C., but work with me here). You have a dialogue with him and his quotation, 'Is freedom anything else than the right to live as we wish? Nothing else.' What do you say from the Scriptures?

2. The late John R. W. Stott said, 'Freedom to disagree with the Bible is an illusory freedom. In reality it is bondage to falsehood.'[2] Examine your heart this week and ask yourself, 'Even though I affirm the authority of the Bible, I seem to disagree with God's Word when it comes to _____.' Then ask the Lord to free you from that bondage.

3. Unit-read (read the entire book at one sitting) the Epistle to the Galatians. Take notes on what you learn

---

2. David Lawrence Edwards and John R. W. Stott, *Evangelical Essentials: A Liberal/Evangelical Dialogue* (DownesGrove, IL: InterVarsity Press, 1989), p. 37.

about freedom in that letter. And share your notes with another believer this week.

4. PRAYER So, how do I pray for my unsaved friend? We read in 2 Corinthians 3:17, 'Now the Lord is the Spirit, and where the Spirit of the Lord is, there is freedom.' My lost friend doesn't have the Spirit because he doesn't have the Savior. And I can pray for him for a God-given freedom from his sins.

⇒ BLESSING 35 ⇐

The Blessing of an Openness to Change

Every time you make a choice you are turning the central part of you, the part of you that chooses, into something a little different than it was before. And taking your life as a whole, with all your innumerable choices, all your life long you are slowly turning this central thing into a heavenly creature or a hellish creature: either into a creature that is in harmony with God, and with other creatures, and with itself, or else into one that is in a state of war and hatred with God, and with its fellow creatures, and with itself. To be the one kind of creature is heaven: that is, it is joy and peace and knowledge and power. To be the other means madness, horror, idiocy, rage, impotence, and eternal loneliness. Each of us at each moment is progressing to the one state or the other (C. S. Lewis).[1]

My friend Mike—who has not yet trusted Christ as his Savior—reminds me of a number of blessings which I enjoy—or should enjoy—as a believer. 'Enjoy' might be the wrong word for our next blessing, but I am

---

1. C. S. Lewis, *Mere Christianity* (New York: Touchstone, 1996), pp. 87-88.

thankful for God's grace. And I believe that we followers of Christ –

WE HAVE AN OPENNESS TO CHANGE!

I am not overlooking the human potential to recognize a habit or a sin that needs to change – and changing it! Alcoholics are sometimes successful in attaining sobriety. Poor fathers may realize their failures and become dads who really care. Rebellious teenagers occasionally come to their senses and become respectful and grateful young adults.

The Blessing

I'm talking about a fundamental, soul-deep conformity to the Person of Jesus Christ. Moral changes may take place in lost people because they have been made in the image of God, but a substantial reordering of one's priorities and values can only happen to one who has surrendered his or her life to Christ. Theologians—who get paid by the big word—call this *sanctification* (a term which means being 'set apart' for God).

The Bible

We read in Malachi 3 about the Lord where He says, 'I the LORD do not change. So you, the descendants of Jacob, are not destroyed' (v. 6). The psalmist speaks of the Lord in Psalm 55: 'God, who is enthroned from of old, who does not change – he will hear them and humble them, because they have no fear of God' (v. 19). We are told clearly in 1 Samuel 15, 'He who is the Glory of Israel does not lie or change his mind; for he is not a human being, that he should change his mind' (v. 29).

Our God is absolutely perfect. And what is perfect does not need to change. James tells us, 'Every good and perfect gift is from above, coming down from the Father of the heavenly lights, who does not change like shifting shadows' (1:17).

But we're not. Perfect, that is. And we need to change in so many ways. For the believer, a large part of change involves *repentance*. We acknowledge our wrongness in an attitude or behavior or priority, ask the Lord for forgiveness, and covenant with Him to change. Saying one is sorry is not the same as a soul-deep conviction that leads to significant conformity to Christ.

ACTION STEPS

1. Analyze Lewis' rather long quote at the beginning of this devotional. How critical are the daily choices we make?

2. Study the fruit of the Spirit in Galatians 5:22-23. Which one do you need to work on? If you don't know, ask someone who loves you where they think you need some improvement!

3. Steve Maraboli has said, 'Incredible change happens in your life when you decide to take control of what you do have power over instead of craving control over what you don't.'[2] In terms of daily life, what one change could you make which will help you spiritually? Ask

---

2. Steve Maraboli, 2020, 'Incredible change happens in your life.' Facebook, January 2, 2020. https://www.facebook.com/authorstevemaraboli/photos/incredible-change-happens-in-your-life-when-you-decide-to-take-control-of-what-y/2821065447916136/

another believer this week to pray for you – and for that change.

4. PRAYER So, how do I pray for my unsaved friend? I show by my life some changes which Jesus is making in me – and I give Him the credit! And I pray for my friend, not that he would try to be 'better', but that he would come to repentance and trust the Savior who does not change.

✤ BLESSING 36 ✦

The Blessing of a Biblical Understanding of the Devil

I have no special regard for Satan; but I can at least claim that I have no prejudice against him. It may even be that I lean a little his way, on account of his not having a fair show. All religions issue bibles against him, and say the most injurious things about him, but we never hear his side (Mark Twain).[1]

'You believe in the devil? *Really?*' 'Yes!', we might answer our unbelieving friends. The Bible is crystal clear in its teaching about a supernatural enemy by the name of Satan, or Lucifer, or the devil. And we believers in Jesus –

WE HAVE A BIBLICAL UNDERSTANDING OF THE DEVIL!

The Blessing

But don't even lost people suspect that there's something behind the massive cruelty in the world, something

---

1. Adam Hochschild and Richard Russ, *Collected Nonfiction: Selections from the Autobiography, Letters, Essays, and Speeches*; Introduction by Adam Hochschild (London: Everyman's Library Classics Series, 2016), p. 736.

beyond the human? How wrong Oscar Wilde was when he said, 'We are each our own devil, and we make this world our hell.'[2]

The Bible

Concerning Twain's comment, I would argue that we hear the devil's side from the moment we enter the world. But we need the Scriptures to tell us the truth about our arch-enemy. Here are several critical truths we learn about the devil:

(1) The Bible is clear that the devil is real and personal. People need to come to their senses and escape the trap of the devil who has taken them captive to do his will (2 Tim. 2:26). We are children of the devil until we trust Christ (1 John 3:10). Conversion is defined as turning from darkness to light, from the power of Satan to God (Acts 26:18). However, Satan must report his activities to God and have His permission for whatever he does (Job 1).

(2) The devil majors in tempting human beings to rebel against the Lord (Matt. 4:5).

(3) The devil is able to sow seeds of unbelief among the Word that is sown (Matt. 13:39). We read in 1 Peter 5:8, 'Be alert and of sober mind. Your enemy the devil prowls around like a roaring lion looking for someone to devour' (see also Job 1-2). He masquerades as an angel of light (2 Cor. 11:14).

---

2. Tweed Conrad, *Oscar Wilde in Quotation: 3,100 Insults, Anecdotes and Aphorisms, Topically Arranged with Attributions* (Jefferson, North Carolina: McFarland; 1st edition, 2008), p. 193.

(4) He prompted Judas to betray Jesus (John 13:2), somehow has power over sickness (Acts 10:38; see also Luke 13:16), and holds the power of death (Heb. 2:14).

(5) Satan wants to sift believers as wheat (Luke 22:31). Christians can give the devil 'a foothold' (Eph. 4:27), but we are to be aware of and take our stand against the devil's schemes (2 Cor. 2:11; Eph. 6:11). He is quite capable of invading the bedrooms of believers (see 1 Corinthians 7:5). He can fill the hearts of believers to lie to the Holy Spirit (Acts 5:3).

(6) We are to resist the devil and he will flee from us (James 4:7). God can use Satan 'for the destruction of the flesh, so that his spirit may be saved on the day of the Lord' (1 Cor. 5:5). Wayward believers can be 'handed over to Satan to be taught not to blaspheme' (1 Tim. 1:20). Paul was given a thorn in the flesh, 'a messenger of Satan, to torment me' (2 Cor. 12:7). He can block the way of believers (1 Thess. 2:18) and can do signs and wonders (2 Thess. 2:9).

(7) Satan's fate is sealed, as are the demons who assist him (see Matt. 25:41).

ACTION STEPS

1. Study how the Lord Jesus combated Satan in His being tempted in the wilderness (Matt. 4). Because He is our great High Priest and can help us when we

are tempted (Heb. 4:14-16), we can follow Christ's example in resisting Satan. Discuss some aspects of that strategy with a friend this week.

2. Read over Job chapters 1–2 and list the truths you learn about the devil and his purposes.

3. I have found great help in reading (and rereading) C. S. Lewis' classic *The Screwtape Letters*. Consider reading this book with another believer and discussing the many insights Lewis has into the 'schemes' of the devil.

4. PRAYER So, how do I pray for my unsaved friend? I don't think I'll talk much to him about the devil. But I won't duck questions about the Evil One either. And I pray for my friend that he would realize he is not yet in the family of God, but in the family of the devil. I will pray earnestly his status will change.

The Blessing of Wisdom in Challenging Relationships

Love is unselfishly choosing for another's highest good
(G. K. Chesterton).[1]

One of the greatest blessings of the Word of God is
that it teaches us about relationships. It is not just a
guidebook on how to get to heaven. The God of the Bible
is relational – and He gives us guidance on how we are
to handle relationships here on earth.

How are believers to live in this world of unrepentant
sinners? And how are we to relate to those who are in
God's family but are engaged in sin? One of our greatest
blessings is that we believers –

WE HAVE WISDOM IN CHALLENGING RELATIONSHIPS!

---

1. W. K. Volkmer, *These Things: A Reference Manual for Discipleship* (Research Triangle, North Carolina: Lulu Press., 2016), p. 253.

The Blessing

In a fascinating passage of Scripture we learn, from the mistake of the Corinthian Christians, both how to relate to those who are lost and how to relate to those in the family who are practicing sin.

The Bible

The Corinthian church had many problems, not the least of which was that a member was sleeping with his mother-in-law (yuck!). And the Christians in Corinth were handling the situation poorly. But let's listen to what the Apostle Paul says –

> I wrote to you in my letter not to associate with sexually immoral people – not at all meaning the people of this world who are immoral, or the greedy and swindlers, or idolaters. In that case you would have to leave this world. But now I am writing to you that you must not associate with anyone who claims to be a brother or sister but is sexually immoral or greedy, an idolater or slanderer, a drunkard or swindler. Do not even eat with such people. What business is it of mine to judge those outside the church? Are you not to judge those inside? God will judge those outside. 'Expel the wicked person from among you' (1 Cor. 5:9-12).

The Corinthians had misunderstood Paul and were committing two serious errors. First, they read his words 'not to associate with sexually immoral people' (v. 9) and thought he meant they were to isolate themselves from lost sinners. Paul corrects them and says if he had meant that, they would have to leave the world! And that would, of course, ruin evangelism.

Second, they assumed that they could tolerate sinning Christians. Paul corrects them by challenging them 'not to associate' (notice this second use of this expression) with a sinning, unrepentant believer, but rather excommunicate them until they turn from their sin. Tolerating sinning, unrepentant believers ruins discipleship.

So, these two areas of relationships—with unbelievers and with rebellious believers—are tackled in this passage. We are to care so deeply about lost people that we will put up with their sin so we can lead them to the Savior. And we will care so intensely for wayward believers that we will refuse to fellowship with them until they have turned from their sin.

ACTION STEPS

1. We believers are not in the behavior modification business for unbelievers. Our unsaved friends may do many things that are sinful, but we muddy the gospel if we only try to help them clean up their lives. We are to tolerate sinning lost people. That means spending time with them. Name one unbeliever with whom you can spend some time this week and simply be with them.

2. We are to isolate ourselves from sinning, unrepentant believers. This means we are to support our local church's leadership when they have to exercise spiritual discipline. Pray each day this week for your leaders that they would have wisdom in dealing with believers who have fallen and refuse to turn back to the Lord.

3. Chapter 8 of my *When Temptation Strikes: Gaining Victory Over Sin* deals specifically with church discipline. Read over that chapter with a friend this week.

4. PRAYER So, how do I pray for my lost friend? It might be difficult to explain to him these two principles of toleration toward unsaved sinners and isolation from sinning, unrepentant believers, but we should be prepared to do so if the occasion calls for it. I should pray for my friend to understand God's wisdom in such relationships and that he would want to join the family of God that cares that much.

✣ BLESSING 38 ✣

The Blessing of a Proper Self-Love

You deserve to be with somebody who makes you happy. Somebody who doesn't complicate your life. Somebody who won't hurt you (Anonymous).[1]

The wisdom of this world, says Paul in 1 Corinthians 3:19, 'is foolishness in God's sight.' Our minds and hearts are fogged over by untruth of our culture. Is our highest goal in life happiness? Lives that are uncomplicated? The complete absence of pain?

Believers in Jesus have the great gift of God's Word to teach them. And the blessing we are considering is that –

WE HAVE THE BLESSING OF A PROPER SELF-LOVE!

The Blessing
The Word of God answers the question 'How am I to love myself?' Erma Bombeck read the book *How to Be Your*

---

1. Grey's Anatomy, season 3, episode 4, 'What I Am,' directed by Shonda Rhimes, aired Oct 13, 2006, on ABC.

Own Best Friend, went out and gained twenty pounds and said 'I haven't trusted myself since!' God's Word teaches us how to love ourselves.

The Bible

The Lord Jesus says in Luke 14, 'If anyone comes to me and does not hate father and mother, wife and children, brothers and sisters—yes, even their own life—such a person cannot be my disciple' (v. 26). Self-love? Here is a kind of self-hatred! Our love for the Lord should be so overwhelming that our love for our family (and for ourselves) should look like hate. Only an unbelieving critic of Christianity will miss Jesus' clear use of hyperbole in this passage.

But what about the Apostle Paul's statement in Romans 7:21-24? There we read –

> So I find this law at work: Although I want to do good, evil is right there with me. For in my inner being I delight in God's law; but I see another law at work in me, waging war against the law of my mind and making me a prisoner of the law of sin at work within me. What a wretched man I am!

Paul's self-diagnosis ('What a wretched man I am!') expresses his struggle to delight in God's law and to turn away from the law of sin. This, too, is a kind of self-love. In the words of Charles Wesley (*Jesus If Still Thou Art Today*) we need to be 'self-abhorr'd' rather than self-absorbed.

Challenging men to love their wives, Paul writes in Ephesians 5 that it is natural to care for one's own physical needs. It is unnatural to hate one's body. 'Each one of you also must love his wife as he loves himself, and the wife must respect her husband' (v. 33).

We read in Matthew 22:36-40 the following conversation –

> Teacher, which is the greatest commandment in the Law? Jesus replied: 'Love the Lord your God with all your heart and with all your soul and with all your mind.' This is the first and greatest commandment. And the second is like it: 'Love your neighbor as yourself.' All the Law and the Prophets hang on these two commandments.

Some have taken verse 39 ('Love your neighbor as yourself') and have argued, 'First, I need to learn to love myself!' No! We naturally love ourselves.

C. S. Lewis has written the following:

'There is someone I love,
even though I don't approve of what he does.
There is someone I accept,
though some of his thoughts and actions revolt me.
There is someone I forgive,
though he hurts the people I love the most.
That person is me.'[2]

ACTION STEPS

1. Look up 'love of self' on the internet. Take one 'inspirational' quote each day and respond biblically to what it says.

---

2. Website: azquotes.com https://www.azquotes.com/quote/876705. Accessed September 16, 2022. In *The Misquotable C. S. Lewis: What He Didn't Say, What He Actually Said, and Why It Matters*, the author William O'Flaherty suggests Lewis didn't say this exactly, but something close to it in *Mere Christianity*.

2. Proverbs 27:5-6 says, 'Better is open rebuke than hidden love. Wounds from a friend can be trusted, but an enemy multiplies kisses.' Sometimes we need to be wounded to wake us up to change. Words of truth—spoken in love—can still wound. Can you think of another believer who might need to be wounded by your words of love and concern? This week write out a letter of your 'rebuke' and pray about whether to give it to them.

3. Read over Lewis' paragraph above ('There is some-one …') each day this week and jot down a couple of thoughts about its meaning. How would you relate what he is saying with what the Apostle Paul says in Romans 7:21-25?

4. PRAYER How do I pray for my lost friend? I need to reflect a kind of biblical self-love that puts the Lord and His will for my life first – above everything. Then I need to pray for my friend that he would find what should be his 'first love' (the Lord).

The Blessing of a Forgiven Past

To forgive is to set a prisoner free and realize that prisoner was you (Lewis B. Smedes).[1]

We have already considered the blessing of an assured forgiveness (Blessing 2). Our next three blessings have to do with *time*. We want to consider blessings that relate to the past, the present, and the future. How good to know that God's blessings cover all three aspects of time! For followers of Jesus, we with confidence can say that –

WE HAVE THE BLESSING OF A FORGIVEN PAST!

The Blessing

It is the God of history who can forgive us our past. And He has the authority to do so. We do not need to be weighed down with our historical mistakes, rebellions, and outright acts of selfishness. Our past can be forgiven

---

1. Quoted in Kristi Ling, *Operation Happiness: The 3-Step Plan to Creating a Life of Lasting Joy, Abundant Energy, and Radical Bliss* (New York: Rodale Books, 2016), p. 226.

in Christ and we can move on. Sometimes, we refuse to forgive ourselves and, in effect, act like we're more important than the Lord!

The Bible

We are not making the case that we can simply forgive and forget the past. No, there may be reparations that need to be made, apologies extended to others, actions taken to show that we have repented of our sins and long to move on in godliness. We want to consider Paul's inspired perspective in these next three essays:

> Brothers and sisters, I do not consider myself yet to have taken hold of it. But one thing I do: Forgetting what is behind and straining toward what is ahead, I press on toward the goal to win the prize for which God has called me heavenward in Christ Jesus (Phil. 3:13-14).

Please notice Paul's single-mindedness in this passage. He uses the words 'forgetting what is behind …' The Evil One (Satan) longs to throw into our faces our past failures and shortcomings. We can rebuke him and claim Scripture that in Christ our past has been taken care of. All the iniquities in our history have been covered by Christ's blood, for the Lord describes Himself as '… he who blots out your transgressions, for my own sake, and remembers your sins no more' (Isa. 43:25).

Notice that He does not owe us forgiveness. It is for His own sake that He blots out and no longer remembers our sins. We also read in Jeremiah 31 God's promise: 'For I will forgive their wickedness and will remember their sins no more' (v. 34). What an astounding statement from the omniscient God who, theologians would argue, is unable to forget anything! He chooses not to remember our sins. This same truth is repeated in Hebrews 8:12 and 10:17 (although in the latter it is worded as, 'Their sins and lawless acts I will remember no more'). My past breaking of God's laws has been forgiven and removed from the immediate memory of the God of the universe!

ACTION STEPS

1. We are not suggesting that we won't be tormented by our past or perhaps even need the help of others to move on. We must take responsibility for how we've lived, but, by God's grace, we won't allow our lives to be polluted by our past. Think this week about a regret or an attitude or an action about which you are still grieved. How does Paul's advice in Philippians 3:13-14 help you here? Discuss this with a friend.

2. When someone shares with you a past mistake, either *identify* with them (if you've made the same mistake) or *imagine* with them how painful that memory must be. Use the full force of 1 John 1:9 to encourage them this week.

3. Of course, God's forgiveness of our past is much more important than the forgiveness we extend ourselves. But is it possible to allow our lack of self-forgiveness to negate what God says in His Word? How can you speak biblical truth to yourself in this circumstance? How would you apply 1 John 3:21-22 to your own life? 'Dear friends, if our hearts do not condemn us, we have confidence before God and receive from him

anything we ask, because we keep his commands and do what pleases him.'

4. PRAYER How do you and I pray for our lost friends? We need to explain to them something about God's forgiveness and how He can cleanse their past through Christ! And we can pray that they will want that.

⇢ BLESSING 40 ⇠

The Blessing of a Promising Present

Walk with the King today – and be a blessing! (Dr. Robert A. Cook).[1]

We are taking stock of the many blessings we have 'in Christ.' And there are many! We long for our lost friends to come to faith in Jesus and begin to enjoy the many gifts our loving Father gives us.

One of the gifts He gives us – we can give others! We can *be* a blessing to others. Today. And for that reason I believe that we who know Christ –

WE HAVE THE BLESSING OF A PROMISING PRESENT!

The Blessing

When we think of time and its three dimensions of past, present, and future, we believers have hope in Christ that today can count for Him. Today, we can look outside

---

1. This is the tagline for the ministry of Robert A. Cook, Walk with the King (walkwiththeking.org).

ourselves and ask, "How can I be used by the Lord to be a blessing to others today?"

The Bible

We are working our way through Paul's declaration in Philippians 3 when he thinks about his past, present, and future. There we read –

> Brothers and sisters, I do not consider myself yet to have taken hold of it. But one thing I do: Forgetting what is behind and straining toward what is ahead, I press on toward the goal to win the prize for which God has called me heavenward in Christ Jesus (Phil. 3:13-14).

We have seen that Paul boldly deals with his past by his statement, 'forgetting what is behind.' Forgetting does not mean there are no consequences that come with our past mistakes. But we do not allow the past to crush us and drag us into spiritual inertia or despair. We know the One who has forgiven our past. We've looked at the incredible statement in Isaiah 43 where the Lord says, 'I, even I, am he who blots out your transgressions, for my own sake, and remembers your sins no more' (v.25). He does not owe us forgiveness, but 'for His own sake' He blots out and no longer remembers our sins.

But what about the present? Paul's words 'one thing I do' highlight his perspective on the now. He is active; he has purpose. He presses on. Right now. There is a goal toward which he strives and he is taking steps in this moment to move toward that goal. He presently forgets and he is presently pressing on. Those are descriptions of a promising present.

Paul is neither crippled by a paralyzing past nor an impotent present. By God's grace, he is able to step out in faith and do something about his now.

I heard one preacher paraphrase Paul's statement in Philippians 3 by saying, 'Paul says, "One thing I do," not "there are many things I dabble in".' The Evil One enjoys clouding our vision, diminishing our focus on what the Lord has for us in the present. And we can consciously resist the devil's efforts at keeping us stuck in a demonically-inspired despair of today.

ACTION STEPS

1. As you think about your present life, what steps are you taking to become more like Christ? Be as specific as you can.

2. Dr. Robert A. Cook, beloved radio pastor for several decades, would conclude his radio broadcast with the words, 'Walk with the King today. And be a blessing!' What does it mean to be a blessing to someone else? And how might you be a blessing to someone today?

3. Read *The Blessing* by Gary Smalley and John Trent. Although the orientation of this book is on families, practical advice and specific ideas for blessing the people in your life are provided. *The Blessing* shows how God can transform our lives, especially in families where we have not perhaps received our parents' blessing. Denied blessings are discussed along with specific ways in which we can heal broken hearts in our families. We can *be* a blessing to others. Consider studying *The Blessing* with a friend.

4. PRAYER The Christian life is not just a redeemed past or a glorious future. It looks at the present and says, 'God can use me today!' Both nostalgia and futurism are incomplete without a purpose for the present. Pray for your friend that he will come to Christ and make today count!

The Blessing of a Certain, Glorious Future

If I find in myself a desire which no experience in this world can satisfy, the most probable explanation is that I was made for another world (C. S. Lewis).[1]

Christians have been criticized for being 'so heavenly-minded that they are of no earthly good.' There is certainly some truth to that statement, but I would suggest that many believers aren't 'heavenly-minded' enough. For that reason, I want to remind Christians of the truth that –

WE HAVE THE BLESSING OF A CERTAIN, GLORIOUS FUTURE!

The Blessing

We've been thinking about Paul's three time dimensions (past, present, and future) as described in Philippians 3 –

---

1. C. S. Lewis, *Mere Christianity* (HarperCollins). Section 10. 'Hope,' p. 75.

Brothers and sisters, I do not consider myself yet to have taken hold of it. But one thing I do: Forgetting what is behind and straining toward what is ahead, I press on toward the goal to win the prize for which God has called me heavenward in Christ Jesus (Phil. 3:13-14).

In terms of his future orientation, Paul states that he presses on 'toward the goal to win the prize.' His future is focused on heaven and being with Christ. That prize may well be the hope of Christ saying the words, 'Well done, good and faithful servant!'

The Bible clearly promises eternal bliss for those who know Christ. The future for the believer is to be with Christ forever, the One of whom the psalmist wrote, 'You make known to me the path of life; you will fill me with joy in your presence, with eternal pleasures at your right hand' (Ps. 16:11). By no means is God anti-pleasure and we look forward to eternity with Him.

The Bible

God's Word tells us a great deal about our eternal home. Jesus encourages us in John 14 to think about the home Christ is preparing for us. We then read, 'And if I go and prepare a place for you, I will come back and take you to be with me that you also may be where I am' (v. 3).

The Father's house is spacious; there is plenty of room. And He is preparing places for His followers. On Jesus' calendar is the day marked when He will return for His people, for His desire is that we would be where He is.

When you feel alone or abandoned, remind yourself that Jesus wants to spend eternity … with you! And if that overarching, massive truth gets a hold of you, there is no telling what God can do in your life right now and in the future.

There have been many bogus 'trips to heaven' type books in the last few years. Some have been debunked; others seem to try to replace the Bible as our authority on heaven. However, there is one account which can be trusted and it is the Apostle Paul's trip to heaven described in 2 Corinthians 12.

Although there is much in this chapter to consider (especially the issue of Paul's 'thorn in the flesh'), we learn from 2 Corinthians 12 two truths about heaven: (1) The sounds of heaven will be 'inexpressible' and are described as 'things that no one is permitted to tell' (v. 4). And (2) The sights of heaven will involve 'surpassingly great revelations' (v. 7).

Scripture has much to teach us about heaven, but its greatest attraction will not be the streets of gold or the pearly gates. The primary feature will be the Son of God Himself, who gave His life for us.

ACTION STEPS

1. I grew up thinking that I would live in the clouds forever with Jesus, taking harp lessons. But the Lord will come and make His dwelling with us in the new heavens and the new earth (2 Pet. 3; Rev. 21; Isa. 11, 65, 66). Read one of those chapters each day this week taking some notes on where we will live forever.

2. This week, think about this statement from C. S. Lewis: 'If I find in myself a desire which no experience in this world can satisfy, the most probable explanation

is that I was made for another world.' How might you use this statement to share the gospel with your lost friend?

3. Consider reading the excellent book by Randy Alcorn entitled *Heaven: A Comprehensive Guide to Everything the Bible Says About Our Eternal Home*. And yes, I've written a short book that is out of print entitled: *Heaven: Thinking Now about Forever.*

4. PRAYER Don't be afraid to talk to your lost friend about heaven. Pray that he would think about the life after this life and how only Christ can guarantee an eternity with God.

⤜ BLESSING 42 ⤛

The Blessing of Reordered Desires

Our Lord finds our desires not too strong, but too weak. We are half-hearted creatures, fooling about with drink, sex and ambition when infinite joy is offered us, like an ignorant child who wants to go on making mud pies in a slum because he cannot imagine what is meant by the offer of a holiday at the sea. We are far too easily pleased (C. S. Lewis).[1]

As a young believer, I remember memorizing Psalm 23 in the King James and being greatly puzzled by the very first verse: 'The Lord is my Shepherd, *I shall not want.*' 'Not want'? Anything? Are all my desires wrong? Am I to live a desire-free life?

Finally, someone explained to me that in Elizabethan language the expression 'I shall not want' means 'I shall not *lack.*' That helped a great deal for I realized that our lives can be filled with godly desires. Therefore, believers –

---

1. 'The Weight of Glory,' by C. S. Lewis. Preached originally as a sermon in the Church of St Mary the Virgin, Oxford, on June 8, 1942: published in THEOLOGY, November, 1941, and by the S.P.C.K.

WE HAVE THE BLESSING OF REORDERED DESIRES!

The Blessing

We all come into this world filled with desires both good and evil. Made in God's image, every person has proper longings as well as sinful inclinations. Conversion begins an internal journey of discovering what pleases the Lord. Every day we are in an exchange of our desires ... for His!

The Bible

God's Word tells us that, prior to conversion, we were marked by 'evil human desires' (1 Pet. 4:2). We were 'gratifying the cravings of our flesh and following its desires and thoughts. ... and were by nature deserving of wrath' (Eph. 2:3). Unbelievers are 'trapped by evil desires' (Prov. 11:6).

Our 'old self ... is being corrupted by its deceitful desires' (Eph. 4:22). Our ability to hear and obey God's Word is at stake, for we read that 'the worries of this life, the deceitfulness of wealth and the desires for other things come in and choke the word, making it unfruitful' (Mark 4:19). Opposition to Jesus is carrying out the devil's desires (John 8:44). God sometimes gives up on a person, for Romans 1:24 says, 'Therefore God gave them over in the sinful desires of their hearts to sexual impurity for the degrading of their bodies with one another.' The longing to get rich leads into a 'trap and into many foolish and harmful desires that plunge people into ruin and destruction' (1 Tim. 6:9).

We are to 'flee the evil desires of youth' (2 Tim. 2:22), to execute 'whatever belongs to [our] earthly nature: sexual immorality, impurity, lust, evil desires and greed' (Col. 3:5). Those who belong to Christ Jesus 'have crucified the flesh with its passions and desires' (Gal. 5:24).

If we choose not to gratify the desires of the flesh (Gal. 5:16), we will have our mind set on what the Spirit desires (Rom. 8:5), and will not let sin reign in us to obey its evil desires (Rom. 6:12). We must 'abstain from sinful desires, which wage war against your soul' (1 Pet. 2:11; James 4:1). We read that 'the world and its desires pass away, but whoever does the will of God lives forever' (1 John 2:17).

So our desires before conversion are described as 'evil human desires.' We were 'trapped by evil desires', 'deceitful desires', 'the desires for other things', 'the devil's desires', and 'the sinful desires of [our] hearts.' We are warned about 'many foolish and harmful desires that plunge people into ruin and destruction', as well as 'the evil desires of youth.'

After conversion, we are still in a battle not to gratify the desires of the flesh, not to obey our body's evil desires, and not to give in to sinful desires which wage war against our souls.

ACTION STEPS

1. What, specifically, can we do to reorder our desires? Look up the following verses and share what you learn with another believer this week: Psalm 37:4; Proverbs 13:4; 2 Samuel 14:14; Psalm 103:5; 1 Chronicles 29:18.

2. Read C. S. Lewis' quotation each day this week and jot down your thoughts. How might we in our churches produce followers with *stronger* (not weaker) desires? Discuss this question with a friend this week.

3. John Boykin's book, *The Gospel of Coincidence*, is helpful in regard to affirming the role of good decisions based on godly desires. Consider reading that book and discussing it with a small group in your church.

4. PRAYER How should I pray for my lost friend? I pray that he would see in me a desire for godly desires, that he would observe the changes that Christ is making in my life, and that he would long to know the Lord.

→ BLESSING 43 ←

The Blessing of Redemptive Repentance

A famous rabbi was asked: 'When is the best time in a man's life for him to repent?' The rabbi replied, 'Repent the day before your death!'

We are counting our blessings as we think about those who are not yet believers and so haven't received what we have received. Pausing to ask, 'What do I really have as a Christian?', is a worthy exercise. *And some blessings might need more highlighting and explanation for us in the family of God.* For that reason, I believe that we followers of Jesus –

WE HAVE THE BLESSING OF REDEMPTIVE REPENTANCE!

The Blessing

Whatever is meant by 'redemptive repentance'? Being members of God's family through the finished work of Christ means that we can, at any moment, recognize whatever sin we find in our lives, turn away from that sin by repentance, and move on in the Christian life.

The Bible

Repentance, in many ways, seems to be an aspect of the Christian life which has been marginalized, forgotten, perhaps even thought of as unnecessary (except for initial salvation). There have even been some Christians who have said that repentance isn't even necessary for initial salvation (but such a position is contradicted by passages such as: Mark 1:15; Ezek. 18:32; Acts 5:31; 11:18; 20:21; 2 Cor. 7:10; etc.).

It is said that a very cautious clergyman in Detroit once challenged his congregation with these words: 'Dearly beloved, unless you repent of your sins in a measure, and become converted in a degree, you will, I regret to say, be damned to a more or less extent.'

But the Bible has much to say about repentance – and its importance! Here are some truths that leap out at me from God's Word: (1) Repentance is a gift granted by God (Acts 11:18; 2 Tim. 2:25). Romans 2:4 asks a very critical question: 'Or do you show contempt for the riches of his kindness, forbearance and patience, not realizing that God's kindness is intended to lead you to repentance?' (2) God's desire is that all repent of their sins and come to Christ (Acts 2:38; Ezek. 18:32; Luke 13:3; Acts 17:30; 2 Pet. 3:9). The story of the prodigal son tells us that the angels rejoice over a sinner who repents (Luke 15:7). (3) Repentance is required for the forgiveness of sins (Acts 2:38; 5:31; 17:30) and for the understanding of God's truth (2 Tim. 2:25). (4) Repentance is for believers who recognize and turn from their sins (2 Tim. 2:25; Rev. 2 and 3). (5)

Both saved and unsaved may choose to turn away from repentance and will subsequently receive God's judgment (Isa. 30:15; Ezek. 18:30; Rev. 2:21-22; 9:20; 16:9, 11).

ACTION STEPS

1. Should repentance be a daily exercise for the believer? Discuss this question with a friend. How does the Lord's Prayer relate to this question?

> Our Father which art in heaven,
> Hallowed be thy name.
> Thy kingdom come, Thy will be done in earth,
> as it is in heaven.
> Give us this day our daily bread.
> And forgive us our debts, as we forgive our debtors.
> And lead us not into temptation, but deliver us from evil:
> For thine is the kingdom, and the power, and the
> glory, for ever. Amen.' (Matt. 6:9-13 KJV)

2. Write out a prayer of repentance for something you have done or thought or felt. You need not share this with anyone except the Lord. Be specific about your sin and research which verses in Scripture help you confess it and, subsequently, find cleansing. Scripture tells us to confess our sins to each other (James 5:16) that we may be healed, so you might consider sharing your prayer with a trusted friend.

3. Listen to the message 'What Is Repentance?' by the late R. C. Sproul.[1] Take some notes on that message and email or text a friend on what you have learned.

---

1. https://www.ligonier.org/learn/series/repentance/what-is-repentance

4. PRAYER Share with your unbelieving friend a bit of your story when you repented of your sin and trusted Christ. Don't preach. Just share from your heart how God convicted you. Pray that He will do the same for your friend.

The Blessing of God's Goodness

The greater your knowledge of the goodness and grace of God on your life, the more likely you are to praise Him in the storm (Matt Chandler).[1]

The great theologian Willie Nelson once said, 'When I started counting my blessings, my whole life turned around.'[2] As we count our blessings, we are thinking about our lost friends who don't yet have them. One of the more prominent blessings in Scripture is the fact that –

WE HAVE THE BLESSING OF GOD'S GOODNESS!

The Blessing

The believer in Jesus faces the same trials and disasters as his unbelieving friends. But Christians are convinced

---

1. This quote is from Matt Chandler, lead pastor at The Village Church in Texas. https://www.heartlight.org/gallery/5907.html

2. Gordon Farlie and Chad Thompson, *No One Told Me There Would Be Days Like This: A Practical Guide to Teaching* (Altona, MB: Friesen Press, 2021), p. 71.

that 'God is good – all the time!' In our present culture in which many people think they can 'self-identify,' the Lord identifies Himself in Exodus 34 with the following words – 'The LORD, the LORD God, merciful and gracious, longsuffering, and abounding in goodness and truth' (v. 6 KJV).

The Bible

The theme of God's goodness seems to saturate God's Word. The devil challenges God's goodness at the very beginning of creation (Gen. 2–3). He causes Eve (and Adam) to doubt God's goodness, implying that God is trying to protect His territory. The Evil One's attacks on God's character have not ceased yet.

We learn the following truths about the goodness of God in the Scriptures: (1) In Exodus 33, Moses asks to see God's glory and God says, 'I will cause all my goodness to pass in front of you …' (v. 19). His goodness is equivalent to His glory. (2) God's people are to revel in His great goodness (Neh. 9:25; 2 Chron. 6:41), enjoying His great goodness in the land He gave them (Neh. 9:35). (3) The psalmist declares that God's 'goodness and love will follow me all the days of my life' (Ps. 23:6). I learned Psalm 23 in the King James Bible as a youth and I thought that there were three things that would follow me (although I didn't know what the first one meant): 'surely,' 'goodness,' and 'mercy'! (4) Believers ask for God's help 'out of [His] goodness' (Ps. 69:16; 109:21). We dare not use our goodness as any kind of collateral. (5) There is a communal aspect to God's goodness, for the psalmist says, 'Set me free from my prison, that I may praise your name. Then the righteous will gather about me because of your goodness to me' (Ps. 142:7). (6) Those who turn away from the gospel are described as those 'who have tasted the goodness of the word of God and the powers of the coming age' (Heb. 6:5). (7) Our being called into salvation is wonderfully described by Peter when he writes, 'His divine power has given us everything we need for a godly life through our knowledge of him who called us by his own glory and goodness' (2 Pet. 1:3).

ACTION STEPS

1. The obvious question for the believer is: 'What shall I return to the LORD for all his goodness to me?' (Ps. 116:12). The author Ann Voskamp makes the point that 'When you're overwhelmed with the goodness of God to you – you overflow with the goodness of God to others.' How might you overflow this week to others?

2. In *The Chronicles of Narnia*, we have the dialogue between Mr. Beaver and Lucy. Lucy asks about Aslan, 'Is he – quite safe? I shall feel rather nervous about meeting a lion.' 'Safe?' said Mr. Beaver. 'Who said anything about safe? 'Course he isn't safe! But he's good. He's the king, I tell you.'[3] How do we confuse God's goodness and safety, do you think? Has He promised us 24/7 safety?

3. In his book *Your God Is Too Safe*, Mark Buchanan writes, 'Holy habits are that: the disciplines, the

---

3. C. S. Lewis, *The Chronicles of Narnia* (New York: Harper Entertainment, 2001), p. 146.

routines by which we stay alive and focused on Him. At first we choose them and carry them out; after a while they are part of who we are. And they carry us.'[4] If you and I appreciate God's goodness, we will pursue holy habits. Read Buchanan's book and discuss it with a friend.

4. PRAYER Someone has said, 'If God's goodness isn't enough to make you believe in Him, nothing will.' Point out something specific about God's goodness that you've seen in your own life to your lost friend and invite him to rejoice with you in that something.

---

4. Mark Buchanan, *Your God Is Too Safe: Rediscovering the Wonder of a God You Can't Control* (Colorado, CO: Multnomah, 2009), p. 131.

⤳ BLESSING 45 ⤲

The Blessing of God's Sovereignty

If God has done what you think he should do, trust him.
If God doesn't do what you think he should do, trust him.
If you pray and believe God for a miracle and he does it,
trust him. If your worst nightmare comes true, believe he is
sovereign. Believe he is good (Craig Groeschel).[1]

As we continue to count our blessings, there is one
which colors everything in life, every circumstance
we encounter, every trial, every hardship, every joy that
life presents to us. We who have trusted Christ –

WE HAVE THE BLESSING OF
GOD'S SOVEREIGNTY!

The Blessing

'Sovereignty' is a big theological term that indicates the
greatness of God in all the aspects of life. The late J. I.
Packer, author of *Knowing God*, wrote, 'Men treat God's
sovereignty as a theme for controversy, but in Scripture

---

1. Craig Groeschel, *The Christian Atheist: Believing in God but Living As
If He Doesn't Exist* (Grand Rapids, MI: Zondervan, 2011), p. 158.

it is a matter for worship.'[2] To trust in God's sovereignty means we are confident in His character and His control of our lives.

The Bible

The issue isn't whether the Bible teaches God's sovereignty, but how man's free will relates to God's overall control of everything. In the midst of his overwhelming losses, Job declared, 'I know that you can do all things; no purpose of yours can be thwarted.' (Job 42:2).

We read in Isaiah 45:7-9 –

> I form the light and create darkness,
> I bring prosperity and create disaster;
> I, the Lord, do all these things.

> You heavens above, rain down my righteousness;
> let the clouds shower it down.
> Let the earth open wide,
> let salvation spring up,
> let righteousness flourish with it;
> I, the Lord, have created it.

> Woe to those who quarrel with their Maker,
> those who are nothing but potsherds
> among the potsherds on the ground.
> Does the clay say to the potter,
> 'What are you making?'
> Does your work say,
> 'The potter has no hands'?

Both light and darkness, prosperity and disaster, are direct (or indirect) actions of our Creator God. The psalmist

---

2. J. I. Packer, *Growing in Christ* (Repack). (Wheaton, IL: Crossway, 2022), p. 31.

declares, 'Our God is in heaven; he does whatever pleases him' (Ps. 115:3). As we think about God's sovereignty, we must also—and thankfully—recognize His goodness. For an all-controlling God who is not good is terrifying!

The believer in Christ is given the assurance of this truth in Romans 8:28. There we read, 'And we know that in all things God works for the good of those who love him, who have been called according to his purpose.' His providential plan is worked out through human beings. We read in Acts 4:27–28 the following –

> For truly in this city there were gathered together against your holy servant Jesus, whom you anointed, both Herod and Pontius Pilate, along with the Gentiles and the peoples of Israel, to do whatever your hand and your plan had predestined to take place.'

God sovereignly allowed a man to be born blind in John 9 so that God's works would be manifested in his life. God the Son sovereignly allows His friend Lazarus to experience death so that the Son's glory would be shown by His raising His friend from death (John 11). As R. C. Sproul puts it, 'Those who understand God's sovereignty have joy even in the midst of suffering, a joy reflected on their very faces, for they see that their suffering is not without purpose.'[3]

ACTION STEPS:

1. How easily we put our confidence in our desired, envisioned answers to our prayers, instead of in the Lord and His wisdom. This week read over the following

---

3. R. C. Sproul, *Surprised by Suffering* (Ligonier Ministries; Revised, expanded edition 2009), p. 45.

quote from the author Jerry Bridges each day and discuss some practical applications of it with a friend:

> God's sovereignty does not negate our responsibility to pray, but rather makes it possible for us to pray with confidence.[4]

2. Think about the whole area of missions this week and ponder this hard-hitting quote from David Platt:

> A high view of God's sovereignty fuels death-defying devotion to global missions. Maybe another way to put it, people, and more specifically pastors, who believe that God's sovereign over all things will lead Christians to die for the sake of all peoples.[5]

3. Read the classic book by J. I. Packer entitled *Evangelism and the Sovereignty of God*. Consider discussing each chapter with a friend over the next few weeks.

4. PRAYER Pray for yourself that you would trust God's sovereignty when you go through challenges. As Spurgeon put it, 'When you go through a trial, the sovereignty of God is the pillow upon which you lay your head.'[6] Share with your lost friend how God is sustaining you in your trial. And pray for his coming to Christ.

---

4. Jerry Bridges, *Trusting God* (Carol Stream, IL: NavPress; Reprint edition, 2017, p. 108.

5. From David Platt's sermon entitled 'Divine Sovereignty: The Fuel of Death-Defying Missions' at the 2012 Together for the Gospel Conference. Accessed January 27, 2023 at: https://t4g.org/resources/david-platt/divine-sovereignty-the-fuel-of-death-defying-missions-2/

6. 'Charles Spurgeon on The Sweet Sovereignty of God.' Accessed January 27, 2023 at: https://www.gospelrelevance.com/2015/06/22/charles-spurgeon-on-the-sovereignty-of-god/

✣ BLESSING 46 ✣

The Blessing of a God-Given Sexuality

> Nothing has stolen more dreams, dashed more hopes, broken up more families, and messed up more people psychologically than our propensity to disregard God's commands regarding sexual purity (Andy Stanley).[1]

We are continuing to think about the many blessings which we enjoy—or should enjoy—as followers of Christ. When those who don't know Christ live sexually pure lives, they are an anomaly and thought foolish by the world. But we believers have every reason to honor God with our bodies because –

WE HAVE THE BLESSING OF A GOD-GIVEN SEXUALITY!

The Blessing

The God who made us created us as sexual beings. When that gift is abused, personal and societal tragedy

---

1. Andy Stanley, *Ask It!: The Question That Will Revolutionize How You Make Decisions.* (Colorado Springs, CO: Multnomah, 2014), p. 92.

results. Our culture encourages thinking of oneself first, pursuing any desired pleasure (at whatever cost), and defending one's choices regardless of the fallout. God's Word, the Bible, is quite specific in its instruction about our sexual lives.

The Bible

Hebrews 13 does not mince words when it says, 'Marriage should be honored by all, and the marriage bed kept pure, for God will judge the adulterer and all the sexually immoral' (v. 4). Here we have three clear concepts: the honoring of marriage, the purity of the marriage bed, and God's judgment on those who reject His guidelines. We read that, 'It is God's will that you should be sanctified: that you should avoid sexual immorality ...' (1 Thess. 4:3). The bottom line is that we should give all that we have to our Creator, especially our bodies. We read in 1 Corinthians 6: 13, 18-20 –

> The body, however, is not meant for sexual immorality but for the Lord, and the Lord for the body. ... Flee from sexual immorality. All other sins a person commits are outside the body, but whoever sins sexually, sins against their own body. Do you not know that your bodies are temples of the Holy Spirit, who is in you, whom you have received from God? You are not your own; you were bought at a price. Therefore honor God with your bodies.

There is a level of personal self-destruction that accompanies illicit sexual activity. The believer in Christ has every reason to honorably treat his or her body as a temple of the Holy Spirit.

The Bible is also quite clear (contra our culture) that homosexual behavior is an abomination to the Lord. Genesis 19, Leviticus 18 and 20, Romans 1, 1 Corinthians 6, and 1 Timothy 1 pointedly argue against homosexual practice (which is the acting out of same-sex attraction).

The biblical norm is heterosexual fidelity between a husband and a wife. The sexual relationship between such a couple may be Peter's emphasis when he writes –

> Likewise, ye husbands, dwell with them according to knowledge, giving honor unto the wife, as unto the weaker vessel, and as being heirs together of the grace of life; that your prayers be not hindered (1 Pet. 3:7 KJV).

Some Christian leaders (such as Tony Campolo) have argued that Jesus said nothing about the homosexual issue. This isn't true, for the Lord clearly said, 'For this reason a man will leave his father and mother and be united to his wife, and the two will become one flesh' (Matt. 19:5). That sure sounds like His affirming heterosexual marriage, doesn't it?

ACTION STEPS

1. This volatile issue is one about which the Christian must not remain silent. We are to be a friend of sinners like the Lord Jesus was (Matt. 11:19). Do you have any gay friends? How are you treating them? How does the Apostle Paul treat the Corinthians in 1 Corinthians 6:11?

2. Take the time this week to read the chapters listed above (Gen. 19, Lev. 18 and 20, Rom. 1, 1 Cor. 6, and

1 Tim. 1), thinking through the specific verses having to do with homosexual behavior.

3. In defending same-sex, monogamous relationships, Matthew Vines says that same-sex orientation is 'a created characteristic, not a distortion caused by the fall.' His book *God and the Gay Christian* argues for such relationships. His book is carefully critiqued by Christopher Yuan in his article 'Why "God and the Gay Christian" Is Wrong About the Bible and Same-Sex Relationships.'[2]

4. PRAYER We believers must affirm a positive view of the God-given gift of sexuality. Be bold in your witness without being needlessly offensive as you confront the cultural majority. Pray for your lost friend that he would see the Bible's wisdom and come to know the Lord.

---

2. https://www.christianitytoday.com/ct/2014/june-web-only/why-matthew-vines-is-wrong-about-bible-same-sex-relationshi.html

The Blessing of Righteous Judgment

The gospel that does not warn from impending wrath and judgment is no gospel at all! Jesus did not come to save good, moral, self-righteous individuals. He came to save sinners who were on their way to hell! (Mark Escalera, Sr.).[1]

'You Christians are so judgmental! Jesus said we are not to judge!' I am sick and tired of hearing that misquote from Matthew 7. Jesus' command was that we not judge *hypocritically*.

One scholar put it this way:

We live, in the twentieth century, in a world without judgment, a world where at the last frontier post you simply go out – and nothing happens. It is like coming to the customs and finding there are none after all. And the suspicion that this is in fact the case spreads fast: for it is what we should all like to believe (A. T. Robinson).[2]

---

1. 'Free from the Wrath to Come.' Accessed January 27, 2023 and found at https://www.spurgeon.org/resource-library/sermons/flee-from-the-wrath-to-come/#flipbook/

2. Quoted in Stephen H. Travis, 'The Problem of Judgment,' *Themelios* 11 (Jan., 1986): p. 52.

But isn't it true that we all long for a just universe where evildoers will receive their appropriate punishment and the righteous be rewarded? The problem is that everyone thinks they are in the category of the righteous! Only those in Christ are forgiven and righteous. So we believers possess the blessing of truth which the Bible gives about reality. We have –

WE HAVE THE BLESSING OF RIGHTEOUS JUDGMENT!

The Blessing

We are clearly told in God's Word that the Judge of all the earth will do right (Gen. 18:25). As the psalmist struggles with the wicked prospering in this life, he takes the long view and says that it was not until –

> I entered the sanctuary of God;
> then I understood their final destiny.
> Those who are far from you will perish;
> you destroy all who are unfaithful to you
> (Ps. 73:17, 27).

There are two and only two categories of human beings: Those who can enter the sanctuary of God and those who are far from God.

The Bible

God is a God of justice – and He will cast the wicked (those who have not fled to Christ for salvation) out of His presence (Matt. 7:23; 25:41), confining them away from God's people forever. Psalm 98:9 says, 'He will judge the world with righteousness, and the people with equity.'

The Bible teaches that there will be a Great White Throne judgment for those outside of Christ and the only verdict will be that their names are not in the Book of Life (Ps. 69:28; Phil. 4:3; Rev. 3:5). They will then be cast into the lake of fire to be punished forever (Rev. 20:11-15). The Bible also teaches that there will be a Judgment Seat of Christ for believers and they will be judged according to their faithful service (2 Cor. 5:10). The issue will not be salvation, but faithfulness. Rewards will be given (or withheld) based on one's sacrificial living for Christ.

I came to Christ as a teenager primarily out of a fear of God's judgment. I have written extensively on the issue of final judgment. You might want to read my defense of the doctrine of eternal punishment in my book *The Other Side of the Good News: Contemporary Challenges to Jesus' Teaching on Hell.*

ACTION STEPS

1. When we speak of God's judgment, we need to do so in an autobiographical way. In other words, *we* have been saved from God's wrath by His grace. How can you speak of God's judgment with someone this week with love and wisdom?

2. I saw a billboard advertising a junk removal company that said, 'YOU CALL. WE HAUL. NO JUDG-MENT!' Someone has said that 'the fear of being labeled judgmental has left our culture with the lack of good judgment.' What Scriptures teach that we—and the church—are, indeed, to judge?

3. Read the 18th-century sermon 'Sinners in the Hands of an Angry God' by Jonathan Edwards. It is easily found online. Do we need more sermons like that one today? Why or why not? Discuss this sermon with a friend this week.

4. PRAYER How should you pray for your lost friend in light of God's judgment? Do not succumb to our culture's optimistic opinion that 'everything will be okay with everybody.' It might help to write out several prayers for your friend's present spiritual state before the Lord.

⇀ BLESSING 48 ↽

The Blessing of Godly Attitudes

The longer I live, the more I realize the impact of attitude on life. Attitude, to me, is more important than facts. It is more important than the past, the education, the money, than circumstances, than failure, than successes, than what other people think or say or do. It is more important than appearance, giftedness or skill. It will make or break a company … a church … a home. The remarkable thing is we have a choice everyday regarding the attitude we will embrace for that day. We cannot change our past … we cannot change the fact that people will act in a certain way. We cannot change the inevitable. The only thing we can do is play on the one string we have, and that is our attitude. I am convinced that life is 10 percent what happens to me and 90 percent of how I react to it. And so it is with you … we are in charge of our Attitudes (Charles Swindoll).[1]

As we continue to think about the many blessings we enjoy—or should enjoy—as believers in Jesus, one of the overarching ones reminds us of our internal struggle to honor God in our everyday lives. The blessing I'm

---

1. Bill Hybels, Charles R. Swindoll, Larry Burkett, Life@Work Book (Nashville, TN: W Pub Group, 2000), p. 125.

thinking of highlights much of the Christian life. We Christians –

WE HAVE THE BLESSING OF GODLY ATTITUDES!

The Blessing

Life is full of situations to which we can respond in either a godly or ungodly way. The believer has *the potential* to respond to challenging circumstances, unexpected situations, and unwelcome surprises with attitudes that come from his or her new nature in Christ.

The Bible

How often have you responded to a situation and later thought, 'I could have handled that much better'? Some of the godly attitudes that occur to me are: (1) **Thankfulness.** We are to give thanks in everything (1 Thess. 5:18). One of the characteristics of the man without Christ is a failure to give thanks to God (Rom. 1:21). (2) **No bitterness**. We are not to allow a root of bitterness to grow up in our hearts when things don't go our way. Ephesians 4:31 says, 'Get rid of all bitterness, rage and anger, brawling and slander, along with every form of malice.' (3) **Kindness**. We belong to a kind God. God's kindness provides rain for the crops, food for our bellies, and joy for our hearts (Acts 14:17). God's kindness leads people to repentance (Rom. 2:4). His grace is described as 'his kindness to us in Christ Jesus' (Eph. 2:7). The coming of the Lord Jesus to accomplish salvation is expressed as 'when the kindness and love of God our Savior appeared' (Titus 3:4).

Kindness is one of the fruit of the Spirit (Gal. 5:22); we are to 'clothe' ourselves with kindness (Col. 3:12). (4) **Forgiveness.** So much in Scripture concerns the issue of forgiveness, an attitude of releasing another person from the penalty of sin. We are to daily forgive our 'debtors' (Matt. 6:12). If we don't, our Father won't forgive us (Matt. 6:14-15). We are to forgive those who repent (2 Cor. 2:7). We are to forgive as God has forgiven us (Col. 3:13).

ACTIONS STEPS

1. Have an honest time, alone with yourself, asking the question, 'What ungodly attitude do I need to work on with the help of God's Spirit? What Scriptures will help me in this battle?' If you can't think of anything, ask someone who loves you what they think you should work on!

2. Is there someone you should apologize to for a poor attitude on your part? Confession is good for one's soul – and will identify an area that needs work. It is humbling, but spiritually healthy, to admit a less than biblical attitude.

3. Should we forgive those who have hurt us – but haven't repented of their wrongdoing? Can I withhold my forgiveness until the other has confessed their sin against me? How would you relate this issue to verses such as Matthew 6:12-15 and Colossians 3:13? Is forgiveness the same as reconciliation? Read the excellent book *The Bait of Satan* by John Bevere which is really helpful in this issue of attitudes.

4. PRAYER Having godly attitudes may be the strongest aspect of our witness as Christians to our lost friends. But we need to be with them for them to see how the Lord gives us right responses to life's circumstances. Pray for your witness to your friend – and that he would find the Lord and begin the same journey to godly attitudes.

The Blessing of a Biblical View of Time

The greatest gift you can give someone is your time. Because when you give your time, you are giving a portion of your life that you will never get back (anonymous).[1]

There are so many blessings that the child of God has in knowing Christ. And while it may be true that an unsaved person enjoys some of the blessings that God gives through His gracious providence, many of these gifts are received only when one trusts Christ and becomes a member of God's forgiven family. One gift which helps believers focus on faithful living is that of time. We who know Christ –

WE HAVE THE BLESSING OF A BIBLICAL VIEW OF TIME!

---

1. Charisse le Roux, *Courageous Hope: Daily Devotions* (Ontario, Canada: CLF Publishers, 2020), p. 27.

The Blessing

Albert Einstein once said, 'The only reason for time is so that everything doesn't happen at once.'[2] We who know Christ believe that our infinite God is timeless and uses the sequential events of life for His glory. He values time and our response as time-bound creatures to the collection of moments we call minutes, hours, days, months, years, etc. As stewards of the time God gives us, believers see time as a gift of their Redeemer to do His work and enjoy His world.

The Bible

What does God's Word, the Bible, have to say about time? One immediately thinks of the section of Ecclesiastes where the writer says, 'There is a time for everything, and a season for every activity under the heavens ...' (3:1). Made famous by the musical group The Birds, this section of God's Word lists certain events (such as a time to be born and a time to die) as under the sovereign oversight of God. The term 'time' is used 888 times in the Scriptures, often referring to a sequence of human events.

What principles about time must the believer keep in mind in this life? **(1) We are to be faithful stewards of the time God gives us.** We should be 'redeeming the time, because the days are evil' (Eph. 5:16 KJV). Concerning unbelievers, Colossians 4:5 says that believers are to 'walk in wisdom toward them that are without, redeeming the time' (KJV). As Alice Bloch has

---

2. Vyvyan Evans, *The Crucible of Language: How Language and Mind Create Meaning.* (Cambridge, United Kingdom: Cambridge University Press, 2016), p. 92.

said, 'We say we waste time, but that is impossible. We waste ourselves.'[3] Our time is not ours; we are only the managers of the hours and days God entrusts to us. **(2) We are to use the time we have intentionally to serve the Lord.** Our distracted culture believes it can multitask. In reality, divided attention is inattention to what lies before us. The missionary martyr, Jim Elliot, once said, 'Wherever you are, be all there. Live to the hilt every moment you believe to be the will of God.'[4] This includes interruptions. Jesus used interruptions to do what lay before Him as He served His Father (see Mark 5, where Jesus is on His way to raise a dead girl, but is interrupted by the woman with the issue of blood). **(3) We are to commit our time to the Lord who knows the future.** We are to use the time the Lord gives us to serve Him, to minister to others, to enjoy His world, to rest, to ponder His goodness to us.

ACTION STEPS

1. The psalmist prays, 'Teach us to number our days, that we may gain a heart of wisdom' (Ps. 90:12). Do you view time as your own? If so, confess that to the Lord and ask for His help in viewing time as a loan from the Lord. Review Blessings 39-41 and Paul's statements in Philippians 3.

2. Ask yourself some hard questions: How much time do I spend in leisure activities? How much time do I

---

3. Les Parrott and Leslie Parrott, *The One Year Love Talk Devotional for Couples.* (Carol Stream, IL: Tyndale House Publishers, 2011), p. 1.

4. Jim Elliot and Elisabeth Elliot (ed.), *The Journals of Jim Elliot* (Ada, MI: Revell, 2002), p. 278.

spend with lost people? How much time do I spend in serving the people of God? How much time do I spend reading and studying God's Word?

3. Read the little pamphlet *The Tyranny of the Urgent* by Charles E. Hummel. He describes the telephone as a great interrupter. How do you look at your cell phone?

4. PRAYER Spending precious time with our loved lost ones is really critical. But we will spend eternity with the family of God. Spend significant time with your lost loved one. And pray that he may come to know the Lord of time.

✦ BLESSING 50 ✦

The Blessing of Meaningful Decisions

Good and evil both increase at compound interest. That is why the little decisions you and I make every day are of such infinite importance. The smallest good act today is the capture of a strategic point from which, a few months later, you may be able to go on to victories you never dreamed of. An apparently trivial indulgence in lust or anger today is the loss of a ridge or railway line or bridgehead from which the enemy may launch an attack otherwise impossible (C. S. Lewis).[1]

We are thinking about the many blessings which the Lord has given to His children. One that I know I need to consider more fully is that of my ability to make good and godly decisions. The choices we make truly matter in the life of the child of God. For that reason, I believe we Christians –

WE HAVE THE BLESSING OF MEANINGFUL DECISIONS!

---

1. *The Complete C. S. Lewis Signature Classics* (New York: Harper One; Reprint edition, 2002), p. 111.

The Blessing

In his marvelous book *The Screwtape Letters*, C. S. Lewis has a demon lamenting the fact that God gives His people freedom to make godly choices. Lewis writes, 'Desiring their freedom, He . . . refuses to carry them, by their mere affections and habits, to any of the goals which He sets before them: He leaves them to "do it on their own".'[2] By God's grace, we choose to become the people God wants us to be.

This idea of meaningful choice is highly significant to the believer. Every day we face hundreds if not thousands of decisions. Some are innocuous. Some critical. And what we decide—every day—matters.

The Bible

Joshua rehearses the history of God's deliverance of Israel in Joshua 24:14-15 and says the following:

> Now fear the Lord and serve him with all faithfulness. Throw away the gods your ancestors worshiped beyond the Euphrates River and in Egypt, and serve the Lord. But if serving the Lord seems undesirable to you, then choose for yourselves this day whom you will serve, whether the gods your ancestors served beyond the Euphrates, or the gods of the Amorites, in whose land you are living. But as for me and my household, we will serve the Lord.

Our choices matter. Some for this world. Some for eternity. Joshua could not have made the issue clearer: the Lord or idols. But the power to make that decision

---

2. *The Complete C. S. Lewis Signature Classics* (New York: Harper One; Reprint edition, 2002), p. 189.

rests in the hands of the Israelites: 'If serving the Lord seems undesirable to you, then choose for yourselves …' And Joshua makes the point that they could choose between the gods their ancestors served or some new gods of the Amorites. He then declares without reservation: 'But as for me and my household, we will serve the Lord.'

The frightening fact is that we can decide against the Lord, against His will for us, against a relationship with Him. The Lord Jesus laments in Luke 13:34 –

> Jerusalem, Jerusalem, you who kill the prophets and stone those sent to you, how often I have longed to gather your children together, as a hen gathers her chicks under her wings, and you were not willing.

The terrifying part about human beings is that we can choose to make horrific decisions. Here, Jerusalem—guilty of killing the prophets God had sent to them—refuses to be gathered under the wings of their covenant God. Jesus' longing to draw people to Himself can be contradicted by those made in God's image who refuse to accept His invitation.

ACTION STEPS

1. Do you look at your everyday activities as a series of decisions that you can make? Are you aware that the next action you take holds the potential of life-changing or eternity-changing power? What one critical decision are you facing for which you need prayer from another believer that you would make the right decision?

2. Think this week about a decision you need to make that will advance your walk with the Lord. How does the Holy Spirit fit into that process? Read Romans 8 each day this week, asking the Spirit of God for wisdom as you face that decision.

3. Read Gary Friesen's *Decision-Making and the Will of God* or Bruce Waltke's *Finding the Will of God: A Pagan Notion?* The latter will pull you away from a kind of Christian divination and toward good decision-making. The former is a classic well worth reading. Take notes on what you read and discuss either book with a friend.

4. PRAYER Be candid in explaining to your lost friend how you make important decisions in your life. Perhaps God will use your testimony to cause him to think about the greatest decision of trusting Christ.

The Blessing of Godly Discipline

Too often, we forget that discipline really means to teach, not to punish. A disciple is a student, not a recipient of behavioral consequences (Daniel J. Siegel).[1]

In thinking about the many blessings we enjoy— or should enjoy—as followers of Christ, some are quite positive on the surface (genuine joy, assurance of forgiveness). Others not so much. The blessing we want to consider now is one for which we should be grateful, but often aren't. As followers of Jesus –

WE HAVE THE BLESSING OF GODLY DISCIPLINE!

The Blessing

We've all experienced the toddler in WalMart whose mission at the moment is to punish his parents and to drive everyone else crazy with his tantrum. He's not wet

---

1. Daniel J. Siegel and Tina Payne Bryson, *The Whole-Brain Child: 12 Revolutionary Strategies to Nurture Your Child's Developing Mind* (New York: Bantam, 2012), p. 139.

or hungry or hurt. He's just angry that he's not getting his way. And he is enlisting everyone else into his misery. He is in need of godly, loving, intentional parenting. But so are we. As one writer said, 'The proper attitude towards a child's disobedience is this: "I love you too much to let you behave like that".' What should be God's attitude toward a wayward adult believer?

The Bible

God's Word has much to say about His disciplining His children. The bottom line is that God will bring circumstances (difficult people, challenging events, financial lack, personal illness, etc.) into the life of His child for His purposes.

The book of Proverbs says much about God's loving discipline – granted, several of the injunctions to discipline concern children (such as the not sparing the rod text in Proverbs 13:24). Proverbs 23 commands parents not to withhold discipline from a child (v. 13) and Proverbs 29 says that disciplining one's children will give the parents peace and 'the delights you desire' (v. 17). We're told in Proverbs 22:15 that 'folly is bound up in the heart of a child, but the rod of discipline will drive it far away.' One writer says, 'Children need to learn to take responsibility for their actions so that they do not become adults believing that nothing is ever their fault.'

But folly is hardly limited to children. I have several friends who are foolishly turning away from the Lord. One of them actually has concluded that Christianity isn't true so he's free not to feel guilt and shame about his sins!

Here are several specific points from the book of Proverbs about God's discipline of His people:

(1) The term 'discipline' is joined with terms like 'rebuke' (3:11) and 'correction' (10:17; 12:1; 13:18; 15:10). Who among us would challenge the idea that we need God's rebuke and correction? Often.

(2) Several negative responses are possible regarding God's discipline. We may 'despise' or 'resent' His correction (3:11), 'ignore' His work in our lives (10:17), 'hate' His actions in helping us (12:1), 'disregard' (13:18) or 'spurn' (15:5) what He is seeking to teach us.

(3) The bottom line is that God's discipline in our lives is an evidence of His love for and delight in us (3:12).

(4) There are three consequences of resisting His discipline. First of all, the person who hates correction is described as 'stupid' (12:1). Second, that person is told they will come to poverty and shame (13:18). Third, the one ignoring correction 'leads others astray' (10:17).

(5) Encouraging words are said by God toward the one who responds positively to His discipline. They are showing 'prudence' (15:5), gaining understanding (15:32), and 'counted among the wise' (19:20).

ACTION STEPS

1. We can't declare with certainty when one is 'under God's discipline.' But we should always ask, especially when life is hard, 'Could it be that the Lord's hand is heavy against me because of some area of my life that needs to be changed?' Ask yourself that question honestly this week.

2. We've seen that the book of Proverbs certainly has a lot to say about discipline. The New Testament passage that is classic here is Hebrews 12. Study that chapter this week and write out ten conclusions you come to about the discipline of the Lord.

3. Consider reading through the book of Job at one sitting (this is the idea of unit-reading a book of the Bible). Why were Job's friends wrong when they thought he was being disciplined by God for some sin?

4. PRAYER Does God discipline the unbeliever? Yes, if we mean that He will use whatever circumstances are necessary to bring someone to saving faith. If your lost friend shares some difficulty with you, prayerfully consider sharing some of what you've learned about God's actions in your life.

⚜ BLESSING 52 ⚜

The Blessing of Certainty

For my part I know nothing with any certainty, but the sight of the stars makes me dream (Vincent Van Gogh).[1]

There is a blessing which believers have which drives some unbelievers crazy! But I've never felt that the emotional or mental state of my lost friends should cause me to deny one of Christianity's greatest gifts. Let's think about this wonderful blessing that we have. We who follow Jesus –

WE HAVE THE BLESSING OF CERTAINTY!

The Blessing

There have been some strong opinions expressed against this truth. One writer says, 'One of the few certainties in life is that persons of certainty should certainly be avoided.' Hmm. I guess that includes him. Another

---

1. A. Leon Higginbotham, *Shades of Freedom: Racial Politics and Presumptions of the American Legal Process* (Oxford, United Kingdom: Oxford University Press, 1998), p. xiii.

expressed her perspective: 'Certainty is a cruel mindset. It hardens our minds against possibility' (Ellen Langer).[2] Bertrand Russell—the philosopher who wrote 'Why I Am Not a Christian'—said, 'The demand for certainty is one which is natural to man, but is nevertheless an intellectual vice.'[3] [Do I detect a tone of certainty in his statement?]

But every day we live by faith combined with a form of certainty, right? We don't have to lab test the food we've just ordered from McDonald's, do we? We trust that no one has poisoned our lunch. We may not realize it, but whenever we step on an elevator we are fairly certain that its cables will not suddenly snap and send us to the hereafter. When a family member says they love us, we're pretty sure we can take them at their word.

The Bible

But what is the certainty that is our blessing? We are not talking about mathematical or scientific certainty, arrived at by specific steps or well-defined experiments. No, life is more than a test tube. Our certainty is the highest degree of probability that what we believe is worth believing.

God's Word has much to say about certainty. Granted, that particular word isn't used that often, but the biblical promise is that we may *know* particular truths without questions which drag us down into doubt. Here are some

2. Ellen J. Langer, *Counterclockwise: Mindful Health and the Power of Possibility* (New York City: Ballantine Books, 2009), p. 24.

3. John Greer Slater and Peter Köllner, *The Collected Papers of Bertrand Russell: Last Philosophical Testament: 1943-68* (London: Routledge, 1997), p. 379.

representative certainty statements from the epistle of
1 John:

1. There is abundant empirical evidence for believing in
   Jesus Christ (1:1-4).

2. We can know for sure that we have come to know
   God (2:3, 13, 14; 3:24).

3. We know the truth (2:20). We know that we belong
   to the truth (3:19). And we know what love is (3:16).

4. We know it is the last hour (2:18).

5. We know we are the children of God (3:1). And we
   know who the children of the devil are (3:10).

6. We know who has been born of Him (2:29). We know
   that we have passed from death to life (3:14). We know
   that we have eternal life (5:13).

7. We know that God listens to us (4:6).

One may read 1 John and see many additional statements
of certainty that do not begin with the words 'we know.'

ACTION STEPS

1. Those who resist Christianity's truth claims do so
   from their own worldview. Read over Acts 17 (Paul's
   engagement with five groups at Mars Hill) and make a
   few notes on his evangelistic approach. At what points
   does he express his certainty in Jesus as the Savior?

2. In his book *The Myth of Certainty*, Daniel Taylor
   challenges doubting Christians, arguing that doubts
   are a normal and healthy part of the Christian life.
   Taylor says in effect, 'Don't leave your church and

Christianity simply because you have doubts. Instead, embrace your doubts, live with your doubts, be satisfied with probable truth.'[4] Consider reading Taylor's book. Do you agree with Taylor? Why or why not?

3. Read one of Os Guinness' books, either *In Two Minds: The Dilemma of Doubt and How to Resolve It* or *God in the Dark: The Assurance of Faith Beyond a Shadow of Doubt.* Guinness does a nice job of explaining the meanings of 'faith', 'doubt', and 'unbelief.' Take some notes on either book and discuss it with a friend.

4. PRAYER Pray that your confidence in the truth of the gospel is noticed by your unsaved friend. If it comes up in conversation, ask your friend what evidences he thinks he needs to believe the gospel.

---

4. Daniel Taylor, *The Myth of Certainty: The Reflective Christian the Risk of Commitment.* (Downers Grove, IL: IVP Books, 1999).

Christian Focus Publications

Our mission statement –

STAYING FAITHFUL
In dependence upon God we seek to impact the world through literature faithful to His infallible Word, the Bible. Our aim is to ensure that the Lord Jesus Christ is presented as the only hope to obtain forgiveness of sin, live a useful life and look forward to heaven with Him.

Our books are published in four imprints:

CHRISTIAN
FOCUS

Popular works including biographies, commentaries, basic doctrine and Christian living.

CHRISTIAN
HERITAGE

Books representing some of the best material from the rich heritage of the church.

MENTOR

Books written at a level suitable for Bible College and seminary students, pastors, and other serious readers. The imprint includes commentaries, doctrinal studies, examination of current issues and church history.

CF4•K

Children's books for quality Bible teaching and for all age groups: Sunday school curriculum, puzzle and activity books; personal and family devotional titles, biographies and inspirational stories – because you are never too young to know Jesus!

Christian Focus Publications Ltd,
Geanies House, Fearn, Ross-shire,
IV20 1TW, Scotland, United Kingdom.
www.christianfocus.com
blog.christianfocus.com